THE
Get-Started
GUIDE TO
M-Commerce
AND
Mobile Technology

THE

Get–Started

GUIDE TO

M–Commerce

AND

Mobile Technology

Danielle Zilliox

AMACOM
American Management Association
New York • Atlanta • Brussels • Buenos Aires • Chicago • London • Mexico City
San Francisco • Shanghai • Tokyo • Toronto • Washington, D.C.

Special discounts on bulk quantities of AMACOM books are available to corporations, professional associations, and other organizations. For details, contact Special Sales Department, AMACOM, a division of American Management Association, 1601 Broadway, New York, NY 10019.
Tel.: 212-903-8316. Fax: 212-903-8083.
Web site: www.amacombooks.org

This publication is designed to provide accurate and authoritative information in regard to the subject matter covered. It is sold with the understanding that the publisher is not engaged in rendering legal, accounting, or other professional service. If legal advice or other expert assistance is required, the services of a competent professional person should be sought.

Various names used by companies to distinguish their software and other products can be claimed as trademarks. AMACOM uses such names throughout this book for editorial purposes only, with no intention of trademark violation. All such software or product names are in initial capital letters or ALL CAPITAL letters. Individual companies should be contacted for complete information regarding trademarks and registration.

Library of Congress Cataloging-in-Publication Data

Zilliox, Danielle.
    The get-started guide to m-commerce and mobile technology / Danielle Zilliox.
        p.   cm.
    Includes index.
    ISBN 0-8144-7130-7 (paperback)
    1. Mobile computing.   2. Electronic commerce.   I. Title.
QA76.59 .Z55   2002
004.165—dc21

                                                                2002001990

This is a Leading Edge Press book.

Printing number

10 9 8 7 6 5 4 3 2 1

Contents

Chapter 4: Your Need for M-Commerce 113

Chapter 5: Implementing Your M-Commerce Plan 147

Chapter 6: Wireless Marketing 179

Chapter 7: A Few Words on the Mobile Future 199

Introduction

Twenty-first-century business management is not for the faint of heart. It's like trying to play a chess game in which the rules change frequently—and suddenly. All too often you analyze the situation and lay the best of plans, only to discover that your strategies no longer apply. The most frequent culprit is technology. Although basic business theory is relatively stable, it does not operate in a vacuum. Modern business practice is based on instant communication and immediate information, which are in turn made possible by technology—the Internet, faster processors, better software, and so on. When the enabling technologies shift or advance, then, a company must adapt to the new conditions in order to compete. And right now, we all know how often those changes occur: all the time! It keeps even the best of businesspeople on their toes; many feel as if they operate in a constant state of reaction.

Modern business practice is based on instant communication and immediate information.

Small companies know the feeling well, but perhaps one of the most surprising truths is that *nobody* is immune. Even the most advanced companies—those very people who help create change—can buckle upon a single miscalculation. Think about it. Despite all the competing standards in the technological marketplace, only a small percentage will survive. It's nearly impossible to tell which technologies will succeed; for every new effort, there are a dozen competing versions. And, in a field where standards are tried and discarded within a few months or years, betting on virtually any advance carries a great deal of risk. Just look at the failure rate of Internet startups: More than 50 percent of them go bust within five years. Even more buckle under after that. If we have learned anything in the recent past, it's that technology waits for no one.

The current situation raises a very pressing question: In such an uncertain climate, what can you do to safeguard *your* business? Unfortunately, there's no magic pill or solution that will guarantee a rosy future for your company. Anyone who claims otherwise is mistaken. But that certainly doesn't mean that you should resign yourself to the role of helpless spectator. You can, indeed, actively work to improve your chances of succeeding in the modern marketplace. How? First and foremost, you need to stay well informed.

The great majority of the world was caught unawares by the Internet boom of the mid-1990s. Although a tiny cadre of programmers and cutting edge corporations was able to anticipate the new era, almost everyone else found himself scrambling to catch up. Within a few short years, the World Wide Web had firmly established itself in the public conscious, and it became increasingly difficult for others to gain a foothold. By now, it's too late to be an e-commerce pioneer. But you still have time to get ready for the next leap.

If the 1990s will be remembered for the meteoric rise of the Internet, then the first decade of the new millennium belongs to wireless technology. Although cellular phones and portable computers have been around for several years, we're only just now beginning to realize their full potential. The applications range from the mundane to the life-saving—from buying movie tickets to revolutionizing emergency medicine. The wired Internet changed the way we work and live; the mobile revolution will have just as profound an effect. Soon.

A Brief, Relatively Painless History Lesson

Despite appearances, mobile computers didn't suddenly materialize out of thin air two or three years ago. In fact, if you want to take the long-term view, mobile computing of some type or another has actually been around for more than a thousand years. True, that's defining the term in its loosest sense; it includes the ancient abacus! Yet even the word "computer" itself is hardly a new invention; two hundred years ago, it was freely used to describe intricate counting machines designed by men like Blaise Pascal, or to refer to the people who used them. Such devices were often small enough to be considered portable—mobile, if you like.

Of course, most people use the term "computer" only when they refer to modern inventions—more specifically, electronics. In that case, the birth of our twenty-first-century wireless community can be traced back primarily to two distinct inventions: the calculator and the mobile phone.

The advent of mobile computing can probably best be linked with handheld calculators, which were first developed in the late 1960s. They were incredibly bulky by today's standards—you *could* hold them in your hand, but only with difficulty. It was better for you and your arm if you just left them on your desk. These computers were simple by modern standards: They performed only a few basic functions, and they were powered by inefficient LEDs. (Anyone remember calculators that displayed glowing red numbers?) Early calculators were also prohibitively expensive; it took several years for the average price to fall below $100.

Still, calculators fascinated people. After all, they were the first electronic products made available to the general public. Only large corporations owned a real computer, and personal computers (PCs) were unheard of. Thus, by the mid-1970s, calculators had permeated the market—and they consigned slide rules to the dustbin of history.

Even as calculators grew in popularity, entrepreneurs toiling in another field were on the verge of a break-through. By 1973, Motorola had developed the first truly mobile phone. (An experimental 1946 "mobile" radio system, weighing in at one hundred-plus pounds, shouldn't really count.) Although that first wireless phone can't honestly be described as handheld, it paved the way for the cell phone boom of the early 1990s.

Some people might hesitate to include telephones in the same sphere as computers; after all, an ordinary corded telephone is not normally associated with personal computers. Yet, as the years pass, the line between the two blurs more and more. Phones and computers have become inextricably intertwined in the modern market: High-end mobile phones are currently being built to include many PC functions, and pocket PCs will soon be voice activated. Modern wireless technology is, truly, a marriage between mobile computer and mobile phone.

We have certainly come a long way from those first, ticker-tape behemoths. In fact, the current pace of progress is so rapid that it's difficult to discuss the latest developments in book form; by the time the manuscript goes to press, another rash of products has hit the market.

So Why Should I Read This Book?

Today's wireless market is at an important crossroads. Although the industry has spent the past couple of years just upgrading older systems, we stand on the verge of an incredible revolution in wireless communications. By 2003, a completely new wave of technology will be unleashed on the world; in just one or two short years, today's cutting edge products will be obsolete. It is thus vital for the savvy businessperson to be informed.

Today's wireless market is at an important crossroads.

That's what we're here for. This book is written specifically for small-business managers, owners, and entrepreneurs—it's written for you. We'll tell you everything you need to know about mobile computing and wireless commerce, and we'll do it in clear, direct language. Forget those dense, dry textbooks crammed with programming code. Staying well informed doesn't mean you have to be able to build a WML application from scratch. What you need, instead, is a solid understanding of the current wireless situation—and of the future. That's what we're here for.

If you were late to join the Internet revolution—whether it was putting a storefront online or even just getting your office wired—then this is your chance to be in the vanguard of a new era. Knowledge allows you to plan. Planning helps you prepare. Preparation gives you the competitive edge. And the edge? Well, that grants you a better chance of success.

Forewarned is forearmed.

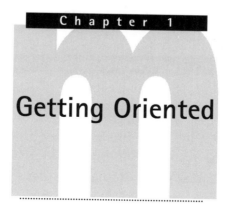

Chapter 1

Getting Oriented

A harsh fact: Discussing wireless communication unfortunately involves using what seems to be an entirely different language. ("Mobilese," perhaps?) Indeed, talking the correct talk includes a positively unbelievable amount of abstruse technological jargon, most of which appears to be randomly chosen three- to five-letter acronyms.

Unfortunately, a large majority of even the most educated public is uncomfortable with such specialized terms. Say your company needs to weigh the relative merits of NA-TDMA, AMPS, and CDMA against GSM—or, perchance, to compare CDPD, HSCSD, and W-CDMA. *Huh?* How can you make an informed decision when you're not even sure what you're comparing? And what exactly *is* the difference between analog and digital?

The Wireless ABCs

To be sure that you understand the basics that underpin our discussion of mobile communication, it's probably wise to describe a few of the most basic wireless concepts before we move on. We'll define our terms in as clear and direct a manner as possible, and perhaps, in the process, demystify a bit of the complex mobile world. Read this section carefully if you find technical jargon confusing. On the other hand, if you're wondering whether EDGE and other high-speed, packet-switched, wireless data systems are poised to capture the global 3G market, then you should skip ahead to the next chapter.

Channel/Frequency/Band/Spectrum

Let's start with the basics. Band, spectrum, frequency, and channel do not seem to be too tricky at first glance. The problem is that these words often seem to be used interchangeably in technical manuals—and almost always without clarification. (Most tech manuals take them so much for granted that they fail even to place definitions in the glossary at the back.) Sometimes a signal is sent over the "spectrum," sometimes through a wireless "channel," or even at a certain "frequency." So is there even a difference? What, specifically, do these words mean?

- **Channel.** Channel is the only term of the four that is not specific to radio. (It's used so frequently, however, that it merits inclusion.) A channel is simply any single path from a sender to a receiver. It can be wired or wireless and can send either voice or data.

- **Frequency.** Frequency refers to the electromagnetic waves that carry information. Each wave occurs, or cycles, a certain number of times per second. One cycle in one second is called a *hertz*, after a famous physicist of that name. The more hertz the frequency has, the faster and narrower the waves.

  When too many signals are being emitted at the same frequency, their cycles match, and they begin to interfere with one other. Wireless companies, then, must follow strict rules governing the use of each frequency—certain frequencies are reserved for certain companies or kinds of technology. The total number of frequencies suitable for communication is limited, so the restrictions create a steep market for space on the airwaves. Competition is fierce, and national governments make a tidy profit selling airspace to telecommunications conglomerates. There's also a push to extend the current range of usable radio frequencies—nobody wants to run out of room for future wireless development.

  Incidentally, a frequency can be legitimately referred to as a channel, because it's a path for a type of signal. All channels, however, are not necessarily frequencies. For example, wired channels do not use radio technology.

- **Band.** A band is a group of waves with similar frequencies. Usually, when companies purchase broadcasting permits, they do not receive access to a single frequency; instead, they receive a region of airspace called a band. The size of the allotment is thus logically referred to as "bandwidth." Examples of bands include EHF (Extra-High Frequency) and ELF (Extremely Low Frequency). Modern telecommunications, however, now refer to bands by the actual frequencies they contain: the 2.5GHz band, the 1.4MHz band, and so on. All communication bands are currently confined to the radio and microwave areas of the spectrum . . . which brings us to:

- **Spectrum.** Spectrum, the largest in scope of the four terms, is confusingly used as both a singular and a plural word. In the singular sense, it refers to the entire range of electromagnetic radiation. Any form of wave or signal, no matter what its frequency, is sent over a certain portion of the general spectrum. At the broad, low-frequency end of the spectrum (ELF), waves are measured in kiloherz (kHz); at the other extreme, where waves are narrower and faster (EHF), the frequencies are measured in gigahertz (GHz). Current wireless communication usually takes place in either the GHz or MHz (megahertz) regions.

    Finally, as mentioned before, spectrum can also

be used as a plural word. It generally refers to the group of frequencies that a particular company uses. So don't be surprised if you see a sentence that contains the words "spectrum are."

Cellular Communication Systems

Until recently, the term *cellular technology* virtually always referred to wireless phone systems. Today, many other wireless devices also employ this technology, but it's easiest to describe the structure using phones as an example.

Before the advent of cellular technology, wireless communication was extremely limited in scope. Essentially, there were only two options: with or without a single base station. Some devices simply transmitted directly from one to the other, with no intermediate station. They were generally used for private communication that included only the parties with special handsets. Walkie-talkies, those popular personal radios, are a prime example. Other than direct reception, people could also make use of a single base station. In this case, the signal travels from the handset of one person to the base station, then is transmitted from the base station to the intended receiver. As the sender or receiver moves farther away, the signal becomes increasingly weaker. Eventually, it dies completely. This situation places strict limits on the effective range of mobile phones, and thus on the utility of the phones themselves. Wireless phone use didn't become widespread until technology could drastically reduce such restrictions.

The cellular system provided the breakthrough needed for long-distance wireless communication. Bell Laboratories created and implemented the first modern cellular network in 1982; its main innovation was the use of multiple base stations, all of which could both receive and transmit signals in any direction. The coverage for each base station is called a *cell*, which then lends its name to the technology itself. It uses low-power transmitters, which allows the company to locate the installations fairly close together, thus improving coverage. To keep the cells from disrupting each other's signals, each cell station operates on a frequency distinct from those in surrounding cells. That particular frequency is then repeated only in areas that are located so far away that they couldn't possibly interfere with each other.

In a cellular network, the user makes a call, which is sent directly to the nearest transmitter in the cell. The transmitter can either then pass the call to the wired public telephone network or pass the signal from cell to cell until the signal reaches the intended recipient. If that seems complicated, it gets even worse when you consider that many, if not most, mobile phone users are, well, mobile when using them. If the caller's signal is being sent to a particular transmitter, what happens if the caller is driving? When the driver goes out of range, won't the signal eventually die?

Cellular companies therefore invented a technique called the *handoff*, which basically involves a cell passing an ongoing signal to another cell as the caller crosses the established boundaries. It's an incredibly complex process that requires many cells to analyze the changing strength of every signal, to determine whether or not to pass or receive the calls, and, if so, when. There are two main kinds of handoff: hard and soft.

- **Hard.** Hard handoffs aren't the best option, but they are by far easier to accomplish. In a hard handoff, both cells wait for the exact moment when the user is expected to cross the boundary between them. Then the passing cell cuts its connection just before the receiving cell makes one. The problem with this type of pass is that calls are frequently "dropped."

- **Soft.** Soft handoffs are the best kind. In this situation, the station about to pass the call waits for the other cell to establish its own connection first.

Latency

Latency is a very bad thing in telecommunications. It refers to the delay between the time a signal is generated and sent and the time it is interpreted by the receiver. Generally speaking, latency varies inversely with the width of a particular band. If a system has high (or lots of) bandwidth, then the signal flows relatively freely and latency is low. On the other hand, if the bandwidth is narrow, then latency shoots up dramatically. Just imagine trying to squeeze rush-hour Los Angeles traffic through a two-lane tunnel. It obviously would create nightmarish delays for pretty much anyone involved! That's latency.

The wireless world struggles far more with latency than does wired technology. One reason is that wireless technology is more complex; data have to go through more steps from generation to interpretation, and that takes time. Mobile tech is also newer, and technicians have simply had less time to perfect the process.

Spread Spectrum

Spread spectrum is a term used to refer directly to wireless broadcasting. Back during the closing years of World War II, the military sought a way to prevent eavesdroppers from intercepting and reading top-secret messages. Broadcasting in code helped, but with national security at stake, the military wanted additional protection. The spread spectrum technique fit the bill.

Spread spectrum is a method of using a large number of different frequencies over a wide spectrum when sending just a single message. Although the original intent of spread spectrum was to deter eavesdroppers, it was soon valued more for its ability to minimize interference. The earliest type was called FHSS, or Frequency Hopping Spread Spectrum; the most advanced type is Direct Sequence Spread Spectrum (DSSS).

- **Frequency Hopping Spread Spectrum.** In the FHSS system, the sender jumps a single message across a number of frequencies during transmission, moving from one to another at seemingly haphazard intervals. There is a method to the radio madness, however. The sender decides the exact duration of each hop in advance, by using a pattern produced by a random-number generator. This information is then shared only with the receiver, who can adjust his equipment accordingly. Anyone trying to listen in is thus presented with an apparent jumble of meaningless radio fragments, or noise. In the first place, the eavesdropper may be unaware that a broadcast is even taking place; in the second, even if the eavesdropper knows that a transmission has been sent, she lacks the necessary knowledge to track the message as it darts from frequency to frequency. Hops usually occur several times per second, leaving would-be eavesdroppers far behind. FHSS was the first system to be adapted because it focuses on mainly on security, which was the main concern at the time spread spectrum was developed.

• **Direct Sequence Spread Spectrum.** DSSS is the other type of spread spectrum technology. It's newer, and currently far more popular than its older sibling. Rather than send a single transmission over a number of different frequencies, DSSS splits the message into pieces, then sends numerous carbon copies of *each piece* simultaneously over many frequencies. It's like a wireless blitzkrieg. Each transmission is specially coded to distinguish it from other signals on the band; the receiver simply needs to focus on that particular code signature.

DSSS broadcasts are singularly resistant to interference. Since each signal piece is backed up by multiple copies on other frequencies, the receiver will get at least one copy of each part of the signal intact. If Piece D is sent along five different channels, then even if interference destroys four copies, one will still survive. All the receiver needs to do at that point is to reconstruct the signal and pass it along.

Although DSSS requires a wide band of channels in order to function, it actually isn't much of a space hog. Since each signal has a unique code, multiple signals can share the same frequency without interfering with one another. DSSS is thus becoming increasingly popular as the airwaves grow ever more crowded.

Circuit Switching

Circuit switching is the traditional telecommunications method of transmitting signals. It's used by the worldwide telephone system, as well as by most cellular phone systems. When any communications channel is opened between two parties—no matter what the frequency or time allotted—access is restricted to the sender and the receiver only. Think of it as a private road, devoted strictly to that single transmission.

Packet-Switching

Packet-switching is a mainstay of modern Internet technology and thus warrants a thorough explanation. Imagine an eight-lane freeway during a city morning rush hour. It sometimes seems that everyone is heading in the same direction. The city-bound side of the freeway is heavily congested; the other side has only light traffic. It's a common scenario. Every city commuter has, at some point in his life, stared at the opposite side of the road and bemoaned the inequity of the lane division. The cars leaving the city could easily squeeze into one lane, leaving the others for overflow from the jam-packed city-bound traffic. At the end of the day, it's the same story, only the roles are reversed. This time, the outbound traffic is bumper to bumper, while the other side flows freely. Each lane is busy only at certain times; at others, the lane is hardly used at all. It's a vastly inefficient system. Of course, on a freeway with concrete medians and real-world logistics, there's no way to solve this problem. But when it comes to communications, the story is entirely different. Data signals can jump from channel to channel without causing undue disruptions or interference. Enter packet-switching.

Packet-switching was originally developed years ago as a way to increase data-transfer speeds for the wired Web. When a consumer uses her modem to open up a communications channel to the Internet, she actually spends relatively little time actively downloading material. (Think of downloading as heavy traffic.) While the user is reading that retrieved Web page, or perhaps off getting a cup of coffee, the modem becomes idle. In a circuit-switched system, the modem is monopolizing that particular phone line, but it is not *using* the phone line. It jumps back into action only when the user moves to view another page, download a piece of music, or otherwise request new information from cyberspace.

Computer experts noticed this interesting situation: Web use is characterized by intermittent bursts of activity, followed by longer periods of, well, *in*activity. And, to the communications industry, an unoccupied channel is a wasted channel. Conversely, when a modem *is* communicating with the Web, it is hampered by the limited bandwidth of that single channel. At these times, the computer needs far more space than usual, but the constrictive circuit-switching system is unable to increase throughput. Those experts were like commuters, staring irritably at those empty lanes on the other side of the freeway. So they began to work on a way to minimize that wasted space—and they came up with packet-switching.

Packet-switched systems allow each channel to be shared by a large number of users. The data are split into small "packets," which are electronically addressed to the destination; each is then sent through a variety of possible routes to the designated receiver. Each packet takes the quickest path, which constantly varies according to the volume of other data already traveling in each channel. When one channel is fairly busy, the packets are redirected to more open routes. In this way, each communications route is nonexclusive.

The efficiency of the technique allows for much greater overall throughput, which in turn increases exponentially the speed with which data can be processed. Packet-switched systems are best used for quick "bursts" of information requests, such as page views. For a few seconds, they have access to the massive bandwidth necessary for fast data transfer. Once the computer has retrieved the information, it gets out of the way and makes room for other users' requests. Lengthy, uninterrupted activities, such as streaming video or large file downloads, still tend to clog the system. (Trying to use the other side of the road is no good if the other side of the road is constantly jam-packed!)

A brief note: It might appear that packet-switching is a little like spread spectrum technology because the message can take a variety of routes. But there's a major difference in intent; spread spectrum was created to minimize interference, while packet-switching was developed to maximize the efficient use of scarce bandwidth. Packet-switching also sends a single copy of the message, rather than multiples. When these technologies are used together—in a packet-switched, spread spectrum network—multiple copies of a signal are sent through wide variety of channels but monopolize none of them.

In any event, packet-switching is an attractive option. It's incredibly efficient, and far faster than circuit-switched systems.

Dedicated Access

Dedicated access refers to the ability to maintain a constant Internet connection. A standard dial-up connection monopolizes a phone line along the circuit-switched standard; thus, when a user is inactive for a certain number of minutes, the connection is determined wasteful, and terminated. Dedicated access is provided for by packet-switching. Since packet-switching is able to utilize a number of different channels, it essentially uses them only when it's actively downloading material. Otherwise, the connection sort of hibernates. Thus, a number of users are all able to use one connection, and the added efficiency allows them to maintain constant, or "dedicated," access. Dedicated access is currently available on both wired systems, such as DSL, and on wireless ones, such as Japan's imode.

LAN

LAN stands for Local Area Network; it's a group of computers, printers, and other electronic devices that are all linked. Usually, these networks consist of a fairly small radius—perhaps just the computers in a single building, home, or even car. LAN networks can also be wireless (WLANs) and use infrared or other technology to communicate. At this point, however, WLANs still have a lower data-transfer speed—usually about 10Kbps (Kbps refers to a thousand bits per second). Nevertheless, they've got incredible potential to revolutionize both corporate infrastructure and personal use of electronic devices. We talk about WLANs in greater detail in Chapter 3.

WAN

Now we're talking about the big guys. WANs, or Wide Area Networks, consist of a group of LANs that are all interconnected. They're created and maintained by telecommunications companies. When a person makes a cellular phone call, the phone first contacts a receiver in its WAN, which then passes the signal along various other intermediaries to the final destination.

Here's the tricky part: There isn't necessarily any geographical rhyme or reason to the elements in each particular grouping. WANs are developed around existing point-to-point wiring and wireless networks: They can include users that live next door to each other, in different cities, or even in completely different countries. Don't worry about why.

Wireless WANs can currently move data at a maximum of about 20Kbps. Naturally, that will improve as time passes.

Time Division Multiple Access

As the wireless technology boom grew ever stronger, more and more industries purchased licenses to broadcast on specific frequencies. Experts began to point out that the radio spectrum is not a limitless source of frequencies; if the airwaves became too crowded, signals would start to be grouped closer and closer together and eventually begin to interfere with one another. Continued expansion would eventually be impeded by airwaves clogged with signals. Companies thus began to look for more efficient ways to get more communicative "mileage" out of their limited bandwidth.

Time Division Multiple Access, or TDMA, was developed as another way to allow a number of signals to broadcast over a single band. (Remember that if too many transmissions are sent over a particular band, then they create too much interference.) TDMA works to avoid such problems.

In this system, each phone in use is allotted a certain time slot in a certain channel, and it broadcasts only when its turn comes. This sounds strange, since we all experience cell phone conversation as continuous, but the latest technology is much, much faster than the human ear. (Each time slot is measured in mere microseconds, so it's impossible for the user to notice the interruption!) The "multiple access" part of TDMA simply refers to the fact that it was created to help a large number of users share the same frequency band.

Code Division Multiple Access

Code Division Multiple Access was developed for the same reason as TDMA: to help make the most efficient use of scarce broadcast space. In this system, however, the signals are not restricted to time slots. Instead, CDMA makes use of spread spectrum technology; when the transmissions are sent, they are encrypted with a distinct code. The receiver then sorts each incoming packet according to its unique "address." This technology was originally developed as a security measure, but it is now directed primarily toward the conservation of frequency space.

The terms defined here are only some of those currently in use, of course. It's impossible to discuss and define every single mobile tech term in existence; not only would this book be more than a thousand pages long, but it would also be ridiculously dense and confusing. Still, these do constitute the most central, important industry buzz-words. Understanding them allows us to gain a basic grasp of the current state of wireless technology. When in doubt during the pages ahead, you can always look to the comprehensive glossary in the back.

On with the show.

The Many Faces of Mobile Computers

PC technology is fairly unified. Although manufacturers would have us believe otherwise, there's no profound difference between one desktop computer and another. All traditional computers have a similar form and comparable memory and processing power. Though they differ in the details, they all at least compete in the same categories. Comparison is thus relatively easy, because we know what to compare.

Mobile computing, however, is much harder to place in a single category. It takes so many different forms that it's impossible to make all but the vaguest statements about the field in general. Evaluation is thus incredibly difficult. Mobile computers are built and used for a wide variety of specialized purposes; Web-enabled phones are simply *not* directly comparable to laptop computers. Cell phones have limited processing power, but they're not designed primarily for capacity; similarly, the quality that makes for a great cell phone won't necessarily make a good personal digital assistant (PDA). Therefore, before we discuss "mobile computing" as a generic concept, we must first clearly distinguish each type of device. They're all built for distinct purposes, and all fulfill unique roles.

> Mobile computers are built and used for a wide variety of specialized purposes; Web-enabled phones are simply not directly comparable to laptop computers.

As we examine the field, then, we will break down the term into its four main incarnations: phones, PDAs, pagers, and wireless/Ethernet laptop computers.

Phones

Cell phones are easily the most popular forms of wireless communication—they dwarf all competitors. But their current capabilities go far beyond those of the simple cordless telephone; they will probably be the leaders of mobile commerce (or m-commerce), as well. Unlike conventional laptops and PDAs, they're already built to transmit; there's no need to attach a clunky wireless modem or other such add-ons. It's true that pagers are also communications devices, but the latest wave of digital cell phones have far more functionality than any pager on the market. Because of their unique position, then, mobile phones seem poised to take a strong lead in wireless Web access, as well.

They seem like they're popping up everywhere in America, and yet that's only the tip of the proverbial iceberg. Many European and Asian nations have completely absorbed the technology—in some countries, such as Finland, more than half the populace owns a mobile phone. Such percentages dwarf current U.S. figures, which remain far below 50 percent. Why, then, have some nations been quicker to adopt cellular phone use?

Wired vs. Wireless—Markets and Prices

Probably the main reason is that in most other countries, wired phone service is expensive. In fact, the United States is one of only a few nations that still allows for low-cost local calls. People who want to contact a nearby friend or associate can keep in touch practically free of charge, simply by using an old-fashioned, wired phone; they can then continue to chat indefinitely without spending another cent. And, since Internet access is normally available at a local number, the United States also allows for the cheapest Web use in the world. Barring the flat monthly access fee, the average consumer can spend hours surfing the Internet practically free of charge.

Mobile airtime, however, comes at a much higher cost. It's true that users can choose from a variety of calling plans, most of which provide for a certain number of free minutes. Nevertheless, such plans can be pricey, and they naturally become more expensive as the number of "prepaid" minutes increases. In addition, once a consumer runs out of time, no call is exempt from charge—even local minutes count toward the established limit. At that point, the caller is charged at a much higher rate per minute, for *every* minute that the phone is in use, than he would pay for a wired call. American mobile bills, then, often do far more damage than the traditional phone bill.

This is not the case in most other countries. In Europe and Asia (most notably Japan), wired calls aren't such a bargain. Not only do these governments charge for local calls, but they charge every call at a steep rate. Mobile phones, then, are an attractive option. Many people actually choose not to have a wired phone at all: Why bother paying the bill when one's mobile is both cheaper and more convenient? Europeans and Asians also value mobile phones for their special ability to process data.

The situation overseas thus strongly favors wireless communication—especially in regard to the Internet. Few people want to spend an hour online searching for cheap airline tickets if they are being charged *per minute* to look for that better price. Surfing—a casual, often aimless activity in the united States—is also less likely to occur when the meter is ticking. Free local calling is thus the primary reason that the United States still dominates Internet usage. According to NetValue, an Internet consulting firm, we have the world's largest Web community by far, at more than 54 million people. We also plug in much more often; the average Web user currently spends 11.5 hours per month online, which is almost twice the time spent by users in the country with the next greatest usage, Great Britain. Americans are fairly content with wired access for the time being; other nations are likely to embrace a cheaper (for them) mobile system more quickly. Japan already has adopted imode wireless Web technology, which we discuss in

Chapter 4. And, as wireless devices develop faster and more efficient ways to access the Web, you can be sure that mobile phones will enjoy an even greater boost in popularity.

The Evolution of Wireless Phones

Even though cellular phones have been widely available since about 1990, they have already gone through a series of major technological leaps forward. The most advanced mobile units of today are far superior to those that were on the market only a few years ago. And, as more time passes, advances will occur more quickly—it's going to become more and more difficult for the average business to keep a finger on the world's technological pulse. Nevertheless, it's still important to understand the capabilities of each current mobile "generation."

- **1G.** 1G stands for first generation. These were the first commercially available mobile phones. They've actually been around for a lot longer than you might think; modern cell phones were actually developed in Scandinavia toward the end of the 1960s. One of the first successful mobile communications standards was NMT, short for Nordic Mobile Telephony. Despite the fairly deep roots, however, it took a long time for mobile phones to truly flourish. First, they had to become cheaper and far more effective—and that didn't happen until later in the 1980s.

  1G devices are all *analog*, which means that they

transmit voice-only, as radios do. Because they employ the older, wave-based technology, they're also susceptible to the main shortcoming of standard radio broadcasts: interference. The signals are relatively weak and can often be interrupted by static and physical barriers. They cannot be encoded without cumbersome equipment, so 1G transmissions are generally considered insecure; just about anyone can eavesdrop on standard analog conversations. The American phone infrastructure is currently about one-half analog and is referred to as the AMPS— American Mobile Phone System—standard. Our country has by far the highest percentage of analog phones of any nation in the world.

- **2G.** 2G, or second-generation phones, are the current standard for most countries; instead of sending analog transmissions, they are all digital. First used commercially around 1991, digital signals are fundamentally distinct from analog signals. They transform a standard analog transmission into digital code.

  The difference is profound. Analog signals are essentially sound waves; digital signals, on the other hand, are composed of numeric information. Perhaps you're already aware that computers, at their most basic level, deal with electrical signals—or switches— that can have one of only two positions: on or off. Either the current is flowing, or it's not. Each position is then represented by a single digit: a 1 or a 0. Since there are only two possible numbers, this numeric code is often referred to as binary, and each 0 or 1 was originally labeled a "binary digit." Eventually, the term was shortened to "bit"—which in turn can be used to calculate data transfer speeds. Bps refers to "bits per second"; one Kbps (kilobits) is a thousand bits per second, while the rather impressive Mbps (megabits) indicates a full million bits transferred in one second.

What digital phones do, then, is covert sound waves into bits of this digital code—the sounds become represented by complex groupings of numbers. Digital phones then transmit this code in a long series of pulses.

The digital style of telephony is far superior to analog, though many of the reasons are too technical for the average businessperson to worry about. Nevertheless, the following list touches upon the most relevant differences:

Clearer signals. Static interference—or background "noise"—is a huge problem with mobile phone usage, especially for analog customers. Analog signals are continuous sound waves, as many people remember from past science classes; since the signal can travel along any level within the wave's bandwidth, it is difficult for the receiver to sift out unwanted static. Digital phones are different, because they emit discrete, controlled bursts, rather than waves. These pulses can occur at only two different levels—high or low—which makes it easier to isolate the background noise. The receiver simply blocks any signal that arrives outside the two designated levels, which makes for clearer communication.

Security. Since digital technology does not employ a standard radio transmission, the opportunities for eavesdropping are greatly reduced. Only individuals with sophisticated equipment can translate the code emitted by digital transceivers—and there are many incredibly complex encryption devices on the market, all of which make the transmission even more difficult to crack. Anyone who intercepts a digital transmission is unable to simply listen in; therefore, digital communication is far more private than analog.

Accuracy. Since digital signals comprise concrete numbers, there are ways to ensure greater accuracy during the transmission process. Immediately following a designated word or bit of information, the sender can emit certain information about the structure of that signal—this type of code is called a "checksum." The receiver then performs a quick calculation with the checksum, to see whether the previous signal was received intact. If anything fails to add up, the receiver can tell the sender to transmit the word once more. Obviously, such cut-and-dried mathematical calculations are impossible to perform with a sound wave, which is yet another reason that digital communication is superior to analog.

Data transmission. Because digital phones emit a numeric-based signal, they can serve many useful functions aside from mere voice communication. They can also be used to transmit data, just like computers, because their binary code is compatible with the code of the wired computer world. What makes them even more special, of course, is that they can transfer all of this information without the tangled shackles of cords or wires—and the potential here is positively staggering. Digital is certainly where the true future of mobile technology lies, and it's what this book is all about. Analog is incapable of conveying digital code, so this older technology will forever be restricted to voice-only applications.

Compression. One of the greatest obstacles in wireless communication is providing for sufficient bandwidth, or capacity. As businesses push to send more and more complex information over wireless networks, there is a corresponding drive to find ways to increase the volume, or throughput, of data that can be transmitted in a certain period of time. One of the most efficient ways to increase throughput is to shrink the information being sent.

Almost all of us have practiced this principle while packing for a vacation: We stuff, cram, and squeeze items into a bulging suitcase, which then stubbornly refuses to latch or zip. So what then? We sit on the lid, naturally! By compressing the items inside, we're able to include more material.

Programmers employ the same concept when designing computer technology, and wireless is no exception. By shrinking, or "compressing," the data, they reduce the amount of wasted space and increase throughput. Once the signal completes its journey, the receiver then changes it back to its original form—just like a shirt that pops out of an overstuffed suitcase.

Analog waves, unfortunately, do not lend themselves well to compression, which severely handicaps their ability to perform with a reasonable degree of throughput. Analog wireless users can send a certain amount of information, but they're limited to an absolutely pathetic 2Kbps connection, which falls far below the current 10Kbps rate achieved by digital units. (Compare both rates with the standard 56Kbps wired modem rate, however, and you'll see how much progress remains to be made.) Again, analog works fine for simple voice/sound communication, but it's restricted to that single purpose.

- **2.5G.** The next major development in wireless technology will be 3G phones, not widely available yet. But tech-savvy consumers can't wait for 3G, so they've sought a stop-gap solution: 2.5G. These phones are a kind of modest stepping stone to the coming third generation; they're now available in limited numbers. Although they're more expensive than regular 2G phones, there's a strong enough demand to encourage rapid development. 2.5G phones are generally best distinguished from their predecessors by their increased capacities for rapid data transfer; many of these units can achieve approximate rates of 20 to 30Kbps. Overseas, the advance is largely the result of the development of the General Packet Radio Services (GRPS) system (discussed later in this chapter). Once they have achieved the faster data-exchange rates, such phones can also be Web-enabled and can conform to Wireless Application Protocol (WAP) standards.

2G digital phones are usually considered today's global standard. Admittedly, in the United States, they account for about one-third of the wireless industry; here, analog is still more popular by far. Nevertheless, 2G phones have pretty much cornered the global market—and a wide variety of digital networks are all fighting for a slice of the profits. For a discussion of the next wave of devices—anything that can be called 3G—see Chapter 6.

Current Wireless Digital Networks

Analog systems will not likely play a major role in the developing mobile tech revolution. The heaviest push for innovation lies in data transfer, or links to the World Wide Web; analog devices are simply incapable of performing such tasks in an efficient manner. Since this book is concerned mostly with technology relevant to mobile computing, we confine the bulk of our discussion to the digital world.

Digital tech is currently being developed on a wide variety of fronts; modern corporations perceive the coming boom in wireless commerce, so thousands of companies are working to encourage such developments. The businesses most concerned with the progress of wireless applications, however, are those that help provide the transportation. Because their services will work only within a certain wireless system, these institutions are heavily invested in promoting the mobile standard compatible with their own systems.

Buckle up, because here we go again. It's impossible to talk about wireless networks without discussing two or three dozen dizzyingly related acronyms. We've done our best to simplify the alphabet mess and select only the most relevant material. In addition, "The Wireless ABCs" should prove useful here; if you read that section, many of the following tech terms should make some sense to you. (Nevertheless, if you're not interested in the current state of mobile technology, you may want to skip over the following material.)

The four largest wireless standards warrant a mention:

- **GSM.** The Global System for Mobile Communications (GSM) standard, which utilizes digital technology, is by far the most prevalent method of wireless communication: More than half of existing mobile phones belong to its network. It was established in 1997 by a global committee, the Groupe Speciale Mobile. (Isn't it nice how the acronyms match?) Today, approximately 130 countries around the world have deployed the network, which has captured an impressive 70 percent of the global market. The relative standardization of European and Asian wireless telephony has helped sustain its own rapid growth; as GSM's popularity increases, the less appealing the other options become. Because of this high degree of unity, a wireless caller in Finland can cheaply and easily contact another subscriber in Italy. GSM bridges borders and boundaries, thus making it the dominant force overseas.

Additionally, the GSM standard provides for high-quality voice technology, and its average bit transfer rates hover in the solid mid-30sKbps range. It's no wonder that so many nations have signed on. GSM has crossed over to the United States, but its penetration remains somewhat superficial—only about 10 percent of mobile domestic service is provided by the GSM standard.

GSM is also set to launch a General Packet Radio Services (GPRS) upgrade to its entire system. GPRS is designed as only a temporary stopgap for today's awkward "in-between" stage, when consumers have grown impatient with the shortcomings of 2G technology but 3G phones are still not ready for mass consumption. To ameliorate the situation, GPRS will shift the already functional GSM circuit-switched system to a packet-switched one.

First, GPRS will offer the dedicated access of wired services. Users will thus be able to subscribe to an online service that offers 24/7 access to the Web; it will eliminate the necessity of logging on every time the user wishes to retrieve a certain bit of information. Because of the enhanced capacities of packet-switching, GPRS will also allow for faster data-transfer speeds—possibly as high as 100Mbps. This isn't nearly as fast as the expected 3G phones, but it's certainly a dramatic improvement on existing standards. Indeed, with its embrace of GPRS, GSM is spearheading the move to 2.5G telecommunications.

GPRS hardly has a lock on the overseas upgrade market, however. Europe is a veritable circus of companies competing for the chance to influence the telecommunications industry. Since GSM is so well entrenched, that leaves them with upgrades. The American TDMA companies have been pushing for the Enhanced Data Rates for GSM Revolution (EDGE) standard.

- **D-AMPS/TDMA.** D-AMPS stands for Digital Advance Mobile Phone System, which was designed to be a companion network for the established American analog AMPS system. This first U.S. digital network has found a solid domestic footing, largely because D-AMPS is compatible with the old analog system.

    To add to the acronym-encrusted confusion, D-AMPS is usually referred to as TDMA, or Time Division Multiple Access. In many manuals, the two terms are used interchangeably. So—TDMA, the more common term, equals D-AMPS for the duration of this book. (Don't waste your valuable time wondering why—it's unimportant to the lay person. For example: Even the separate GSM system runs on a type of TDMA technology. Got a headache yet?) Typical speeds on the American TDMA network hover around a poky 8Kbps. For your reference, the much-touted PCS service happens to run on the TDMA system.

    As GSM is providing its new GPRS service, the United States has also created a packet-switch protocol overlay to the AMPS and D-AMPS systems: Cellular Digital Packet Data (CDPD). Although it does enable wireless Web surfing, it provides much slower access speeds than its European competitor. In addition, as of 2001 only about 50 percent of U.S. territory provided CDPD service. CDPD protocol is most often found on modem cards for wireless computers, although many analog and digital services have begun to employ it as well.

The TDMA 3G upgrade, as mentioned earlier, is called EDGE. It can be applied to both TDMA and GSM networks and offers a similar boost in processing power. It will compete for power mainly with W-CDMA. (See discussion later in this chapter.)

Finally, you should probably know that the 3G European networks—which will be based on W-CDMA technology—are referred to as the Universal Mobile Telecommunications System (UMTS). For all practical purposes, the two terms are interchangeable. At least, that's the situation in many computer magazines.

- **CDMA.** CDMA, or Code Division Multiple Access (see "ABCs"), is the second digital network developed in the United States and is the only other serious domestic competitor of TDMA and GSM. Like TDMA and GSM, it is also a 2G standard—but it's definitely superior to the TDMA technology. CDMA supports data rates of about 14.4Kbps and also has increased bandwidth efficiency. (In other words, it takes up less of that valuable airspace.) Qualcomm developed and uses the CDMA network. Because of CDMA's technical superiority, it's also the starting point for the domestic push toward 3G technology. The CDMA system will almost certainly become more influential upon the receipt of upgrades such as CDMA 2000 and W-CDMA.

- **PDC.** Japan has developed a similar companion system for domestic use, to accompany its own analog network (J-TACS). Its digital upgrade is referred to as Personal Digital Cellular (PDC). It is functionally similar to TDMA, though somewhat lower in quality due to differences in the Japanese situation. Yet, ironically, PDC is actually the second most prevalent network in the world. Wireless technology has thoroughly permeated the Japanese culture—approximately 40 percent of the population owns a mobile phone, as compared to fewer than one person in four in the United States. PDC is also popular because of the Japanese imode system, developed by NTT DoCoMo. The Japanese enthusiasm for wireless tech is apparent even in the NTT corporate name: DoCoMo stands for DO COmmunicate over the MObile network. It's hard not to chuckle at such an awkward title, but the technology is incredibly elegant. Besides, there's a method to the seeming madness: *docomo* means "everywhere" in Japanese. Imode phones constitute the most prevalent method of accessing the Web from a wireless terminal. (See Chapter 4 for more information about the imode system.)

  This technology-saturated island is certainly not satisfied with its current success, however. Japan, too, is steadfastly working toward 3G capability and is most likely to embrace the W-CDMA protocol as soon as it becomes available.

Despite their domestic convenience, however, TDMA, CDMA, and PDC are not exactly poised to take over the world. At less than 15Kbps, their raw bit rates are slower than that of the GSM standard, and the voice quality is also inferior. For these reasons, North American and Japanese standards are not likely to find a large following outside their home countries; nevertheless, they'll continue to grow within their own spheres of influence. Strategy Analytics predicts that by 2006, GSM will still hold an overall market share of 55 percent, and most other experts agree; GSM will remain the king of a divided wireless market, at least for the immediate future.

Web Access for Phones

As of late 2001, mobile phones had deeply penetrated the telecommunications market. Close to 50 percent of telephone conversations in Europe are now unfettered by wires, and many third world nations, with underdeveloped landline networks, must rely primarily on cellular phones for communication. Experts even predict that within just a year or two, mobile phones will outnumber wired phones. In a relatively wire-dependent United States, this is hard to believe—but the numbers don't lie.

Phone conversations are one thing, however, and Internet readiness is another. Despite the prevalence of mobile phones, most of the units are still not Web-enabled. Even in Japan, the nation that established the landmark imode service, less than 10 percent of the populace has taken advantage of a mobile Internet connection; and, believe it or not, that seemingly paltry figure is actually the highest percentage in the world. It goes without saying that most Americans are—at best—only dimly aware of the latest breakthroughs.

> Businesses and managers should keep a sharp eye on wireless developments; they will soon be more relevant than we can possibly imagine.

Why the holdup? For one thing, the technology is simply too new to be universal yet; even imode is only three years old. Though mobile phones have had more than ten years to catch on, only the nascent 2.5 and 3G devices are capable of accessing the Internet. Since they are still in the formative stages, these products have yet to find widespread use.

It seems clear that the true ether-commerce revolution is just now beginning to take root. Though the groundwork for the wireless Web is settling into place, businesses and consumers have only recently begun to explore the possibilities. The potential for growth is simply staggering—when high-tech, speedy, Web-enabled 3G phones hit the commercial market in a year or two, ether-commerce will explode. Businesses and managers should keep a sharp eye on wireless developments; they will soon be more relevant than we can possibly imagine.

For now, the world is holding its collective breath. While research companies make a dash for the 3G brass ring, corporations are girding themselves for battle in the mobile arena. Get ready. The revolution is almost upon us.

Personal Digital Assistants (PDAs)

Personal digital assistants, almost always referred to as PDAs, constitute the second major category of instrument in the mobile computing. While mobile phones developed—not surprisingly—from wired phones, PDAs can trace their genealogy back to those first handheld calculators of the early 1970s. Though not quite as widespread as cellular phones, PDAs are certainly playing an influential role in the wireless world, especially because they provide a more suitable environment for surfing the Web than do cell phones.

PDA—A PC's Best Friend

The PDAs of today are essentially desktop computers that have been scaled down to a small size. Generally speaking, they are more functional than wireless phones but less functional than PCs or full-size laptop computers. When pressed for a more specific definition, however, it becomes more difficult to explain what the exact boundaries are.

Suffice it to say that PDAs are always handheld computers, usually smaller than a typical hardcover book. The PalmPilot series, after all, derived its name from its size—the machines fit into the palm of a user's hand. Because of their diminutive size, however, they lack the built-in full-size keyboard and substantial memory of laptops. Some include scaled-down versions of the keyboard, but with keys so small that they're often difficult to use. Many PDA manufacturers have coped with the obstacle of data entry by developing the touch screen; rather than typing in information, the user can simply touch on certain areas of the screen.

Still, modern PDAs allow for many more functions than calculators or cellular phones. PDA display screens are larger—by far—than those of the other devices. They also include hardwired programs for word processing and spreadsheets, not to mention scheduling and other database programs. There is also a dazzling variety of other games and applications that can be downloaded to the PDA after purchase, a process often accomplished free of charge, thanks to the Internet.

In essence, PDAs are designed as auxiliary, or supportive, partners to the standard PC. They can share information with the desktop computer, acting as the talented supporting actor to the desktop star; it's also why they're often referred to as satellite devices. They have the mobility and freedom to travel with the user, and sufficient memory to effectively perform light to medium tasks. They can then be connected to the PC at regular intervals to either upload or download information.

Evolution of the PDA

Although they now provide a wide variety of programs and applications, the first PDAs were little more than fancy calculators. Psion led the way in early development, debuting the first PDA in1984: the Psion Organizer. The Organizer allowed for basic data processing but wasn't very user-friendly. It had no extra programs wired into the hard drive; the user had to insert individual cartridges, one for each desired program. Even those applications weren't all that useful.

Still, it was an important step forward, and within a few years Psion scored another breakthrough; it produced the first truly popular PDA. The Psion Series 3, released in 1991, had a complete (though minuscule) keyboard and a solid array of applications. Such flip-up, "clamshell" devices became known as Handheld PCs, or HPCs. Other companies, seeing the potential of the new devices, soon followed Psion into the fray.

Up to this point, however, handheld computers were unavoidably clunky. No matter how much the technology advanced, no matter how small the computer chips became, the manufacturers still crammed keyboards into every unit. Although each company knew that such bulky inclusions hampered the computer's use as a handheld, typing was seen as a necessary evil. Any other method of data entry was deemed too awkward. The Psion Organizer and other early PDAs all incorporated small keypads. Some companies, such as Apple, tried to develop an alternate system; they experimented with touch-sensitive screens and handwriting recognition programs, but none of them were successful.

The Palm series, which made its first appearance in 1996, was the first reliable device to sport that fantastic new innovation, the touch screen. PalmPilots offered users the unprecedented ability to interact directly with the material on screen. Through the use of a stylus, users could point, click, drag, highlight, type in material using on-screen keys, or even write directly on the pad itself. This last innovation was probably the greatest of all; today's PDAs can quickly and accurately transform an idiosyncratic, hand-printed scrawl into standard words. Palm called the handwriting system "Graffiti," and it completely revolutionized the industry. As opposed to the "clamshell" handhelds, which contained the minikeyboards, these Palm devices heralded a new breed of sleeker "notebooks." Palm computers were so unique that they quickly dominated the PDA market. Today, they still hold a very commanding position in the field, though the competition is building.

The current main types of PDAs warrant a description:

- **Palm.** Palm computers, for now, are still kings of the PDA hill. Roughly speaking, they have cornered around 70 percent of their niche market. Although this is a smaller figure than that of two or three years ago, when Palm was the manufacturer of around 80 percent of the PDAs on the market, much of its business has been lost only to itself, for example, to subsidiaries like Handspring. If you include Handspring's popular Visor model, the 70 percent figure jumps to around 85 percent—which isn't half bad considering that Palm has now weathered more than five years of fierce, no-holds-barred competition.

  When the first PalmPilots—the 1000 and the 5000—appeared, consumers were most struck by the simplicity of the devices: no unwieldy keyboards, no bulky housing to include disk drives and memory, no delicate extra parts. The general design consisted of just an elegant rectangle with a few buttons and a stylus, created primarily for PIM (Personal Information Management) purposes. At the base of the PalmPilot, a small rectangular area was set aside for Graffiti handwriting purposes. That was pretty much it.

Each Palm device since those first models has been designed with the same minimalist intentions. Despite the increasing demand for color monitors, most Palm PDAs are still content with "grayscale" screens, which display only four colors of gray. Colors are great, the company believes, but they also present a huge power drain. Palm PDAs have been know to run longer than one month on a single battery, while some competing brands need to be recharged every few days. The Palm design philosophy focuses on the basics: providing a reliable, streamlined program and a long battery life.

But even though Palm computers were originally designed around small databases such as calendars and address books, the number of optional programs has exploded in recent years. The kinds of tasks you can accomplish with a standard Palm device is simply staggering—you can word process, e-mail, fax, download photos, draw, play music, read e-books, and much more. And, since the Palm VII hit the market in the mid-1999, you can now access the Web as well—and that is the most important development of all.

- **Pocket PCs.** Although Palm still dominates the PDA industry, other companies are gaining ground; right now, the main competitors are Casio, Hewlett-Packard, and Compaq, all notebook manufacturers. (Sadly, Psion's pioneering clamshell HPCs are a dying breed.) All of these companies produce individual models, which sell with varying rates of success. Despite their differences, however, most of them have beautiful multicolor screens. They also have more space for add-ons, extra memory, and all the bells and whistles that so many people love, all luxuries they pay for with vastly decreased battery time. Batteries for these devices last only about eight hours, as compared to the Palm's four weeks. All these non-Palm brands are collectively referred to as pocket PCs because they all have at least one thing in common: Microsoft, the original PC wizard.

  Even though Microsoft made a relatively late appearance on the PDA scene (1997), it quickly demonstrated its characteristic ability to capture the attention of any developing market. Outside of Palm and its subsidiaries, most handheld PDAs are now run by the same OS, or Operating System: Windows CE. (An OS is simply the framework program for the device—the graphics, buttons, and windows that appear as the user navigates through the various programs.) Just as most computer owners have become accustomed to the Microsoft Windows desktop or Mac OS on their home computers, so most non-Palm device owners can expect to see a Windows-like system hardwired into their pocket PC.

Windows CE is a far friendlier OS for PC users. In the first place, Windows is familiar, so it's easier for new PDA owners to learn the ropes. In the second, a large part of any PDA's utility lies in its ability to easily store PC data. Since Microsoft practically has a monopoly on office infrastructure, most employees use Excel, Word, and other Microsoft Office applications on a regular basis—and thus have a lot of work stored in Microsoft programs. Syncing a pocket PC with an Excel file is much easier than downloading that same file to a Palm device.

Palm devices have their own distinct OS (imaginatively dubbed the Palm OS), which is also used by Handspring and a few others. The Palm OS has been praised as efficient and user-friendly; its only drawback is that it can't offer instant Microsoft compatibility. It is perfectly capable of storing converted Excel or Word files, but the process is a bit trickier.

Web Access for PDAs

Almost every single PDA now on the market needs external hardware in order to surf the Internet. You can technically connect them to your home PC and access the Web from the desktop, but in that case you've taken away the whole point of having a mobile experience. No, to telecommute with a standard PDA, you've got to buy a modem. They come in two forms: wired and wireless.

Wired modem adapters function just as normal, built-in 56K dial-ups. Some of them must be plugged in externally, through the serial connector built in to the PDA. The other kind is a bit more space conscious—they're modem cards that fit into the expansion slots of just about any handheld device. Wired modems can be purchased from Palm—obviously, only if you own a Palm PDA. Pocket PC owners can buy a wired modem from a variety of other companies, including Kingston, PreTec Electronics, and Xircom. They generally cost between $100 and $150. Either way, such additions plug directly into a phone jack and thus can't be considered wireless.

Wireless modem add-ons, on the other hand, are a bit more complicated. Palm computer owners are in luck: They can use the Minstrel wireless modem, which costs about $370. Novotel and Sierra Wireless also produce varieties, although pocket PC owners may or may not be able to find a version that fits into the PC expansion card slot. The technology is so new that it's still being developed. By the time this book goes to print, it's likely that more options will be available. Regardless of what wireless modem the owner buys, it's going to be expensive; they also move at the archaic speed of about 14Kbps, which sets the surfer back to about 1995 wired modem standards. Each wireless add-on also increases the size and weight of the device, a drawback that prevents users from permanently keeping the modem card in the expansion slot. Still, they come with the added convenience of true mobility. You can access the Web while in your car or even just walking down the street.

The Palm VII is currently the only handheld computer that has built-in Web access. It has caused quite a stir in the brief time it has been on the market. The Palm VII is only about a half-inch taller than other items in the Palm series, and it has batteries that last almost as long as its older companions. Like the wireless add-ons, it can achieve download speeds of about 14Kbps.

Pagers

As phones become more and more technologically advanced, some people might believe that the electronic pager must be headed for extinction. After all, while the latest phones support both conversation and short text messaging, pagers are usually one-way communication devices, limited to only the barest text essentials. European nations, in addition, have been slow to grant the spectrum needed for the more advanced paging technology. Nevertheless, despite their limitations, pagers are still enjoying a boom market. In most countries, the number of paging devices continues to grow at a healthy rate. Why is this?

Well, there are several reasons. In the first place, pagers are far cheaper than phones. You're not billed per minute to use the device, which is a great bonus to those who tire of being nickel-and-dimed every time they receive a cell phone bill. Instead, users can often pay a flat monthly fee; no matter how many times they're paged, the cost remains the same.

Pagers also have the benefit of "dedicated" communications access—you can leave them on practically forever, and they're always at the ready. In the same vein, the batteries last for a very long time when compared with other mobile devices; if you're unable to charge your cell phone and the battery dies, the pager is sure to keep on ticking.

Paging systems operate on a lower frequency than most other wireless communication. As a result, each designated "cell" has a larger area than those for phones and computers, which means better service coverage. If you're in Boondocks, Montana, your phone probably will inform you that there's "No Service" in the area. Your trusty pager, on the other hand, will most likely still be ready to go.

Finally, pagers have not been entirely left behind by the latest advances in wireless technology. Two-way pagers—most notably, RIM's BlackBerry—have become more and more common, with many devices sporting a tiny keyboard for text input. Such systems, referred to as "narrowband PCS," are great for increasingly cost-conscious consumers. If two people own a two-way unit, they can communicate with each other at little to no charge.

Pagers are thus popular with business employees who work in the field. Construction workers, real estate workers, and miners find that cell phones are expensive to use on a frequent basis, though the nature of their business demands constant contact with the home office, foreman, or even one another. In addition, because of their often far-flung locations, cost isn't the only problem: In remote areas, cellular service might be simply unavailable. Pagers, then, with their better service coverage, are a suitable answer for such people.

RIM's BlackBerry 957, in particular, has found an enthusiastic niche market—so much so, in fact, that these devices warrant specific attention. These pagers are actually diminutive e-mail machines. Most pagers are able to receive several words' worth of text, which is acceptable for only the briefest of messages. The BlackBerry, on the other hand, transcends the limitations of standard pagers. It is capable of both sending and receiving up to *twenty lines* of text—almost a full paragraph on a standard book page. Almost any message can be made to fit that limit, especially if the user is creative with abbreviations. Workers can thus shoot constant e-mails back and forth to one another, even when far from a PC, and do it practically free of charge. There's never the need to leave a voice mail message that the receiver might fail to notice for a long time, never a worry that poor coverage might break up the signal.

The BlackBerry also incorporates some PDA functionality. It has calendar and appointment book applications and can keep track of task lists. BlackBerry aficionados proclaim that this particular device negates dependence on both cell phones and PDAs; it's smaller, cheaper, and more reliable.

The main drawback, of course, is that BlackBerry pagers don't arrive with an e-mail account; the software does come bundled on the device, but it requires a certain amount of set-up. Nevertheless, though they're incredibly useful in certain situations, the BlackBerry and other two-way pagers are unlikely to take over the mobile world any time soon. With work-specific communication, it's usually easy to preserve the necessary brevity; that's why so many companies use the pagers primarily for internal communications. But the twenty-line limit remains, which isn't always ideal for lengthier e-mails from prospective clients or inquisitive customers. A solid percentage of communication is, for now, still best handled over the phone or wired e-mail.

Wireless/Ethernet Laptops

Laptop computers are in a mobile class by themselves. Although PDAs, two-way pagers, and cell phones have their differences, they still share a similarity of size, form, and function. Laptops have far less in common with them—they're kind of in a class of their own. The biggest dissimilarities:

- **Size.** First, there's the size thing. Although laptops are technically mobile, in that they can be moved around with relative ease, they certainly don't qualify as handhelds. Consumers often use their cell phones and PDAs with one hand while on the move, but laptop users are almost always sitting in one place while they work. You'll never see a pedestrian hurrying down the street while typing on her laptop with one hand. Sure, laptops could get significantly smaller—but then they'd be PDAs! There's thus a permanent size difference between the two types of mobile computers.

- **Form.** Laptops may be far less mobile than PDAs and cell phones, but their form is much more user-friendly. PDAs and cell phones—again, because of their size—are unable to support a full-size keyboard. Nearly all laptops are large enough to have at least a scaled-down version of a standard board; users can thus type in information just as easily they would on a PC. That's a big plus. Handheld users are stuck with that stylus, clicker, and/or tiny numeric keypad. Laptops also have bigger screens, which offer a fuller, more traditional computer experience. There's no squinting necessary, and scrolling is kept to a minimum.

• **Function.** Finally, laptop computers have a higher capacity than their handheld relatives. Although they have far less memory than standard PCs, they still have sufficient space for most consumers to run programs, download material, and surf the Web without feeling that handheld pinch. Their processors are pretty fast, and their screens can display the same graphics and colors as wired devices. Internet access from a laptop computer can hardly be differentiated from the desktop experience.

So why include laptops in our discussion of mobile computers? Well, first, they *are* mobile. Travelers everywhere take their laptops with them on both business trips and vacations. The key is that laptops can operate without wires of any kind. Unlike PCs, they're capable of running on battery power. Most laptop batteries last for at least two to three hours, which enables the owner to use the computer pretty much anywhere she wants. You can even take them to the beach. (That is, if you want to risk possible sun, sand, and water damage!) In addition, this book's main focus is on wireless technology—and laptops certainly fit the bill. Laptop computers currently have the best wireless capabilities. Many of today's models are able to both participate in a speedy wireless network and/or connect wirelessly to the Internet. Such uses are far more popular with laptops than with PDAs.

Although wireless technology is relatively new, wired networks have been around since the 1970s. The technology is nothing mind-shattering; they're simply LANs that connect a series of computers to one another so that they can share databases and other information. Of course, this situation—in which computers are equal partners in an interactive group—was likely to stir up a great deal of confusion. Therefore, in order for networks to interplay smoothly with one another, engineers developed a number of standard network protocols. The first and most popular of these was the Ethernet.

The Ethernet standard is practically universal in the modern wired workplace. It debuted in 1974, enabling networked computers to share information at about 10Mbps. By today's standards, that's incredibly slow. Some modern Ethernet networks run at more than 10Gbps, which is a hundred times faster. The system's main drawback is that the connection is public; when too many users clog the channels, the network slows down dramatically. There are two main levels of Ethernet access: 10BaseT and 100BaseT, which can transmit data at 10 and 100Mbps, respectively. These are the standards that currently dominate the workplace.

Yet, though the Ethernet has ruled the roost for a number of years, wireless rivals are becoming increasingly popular. They started out too slow and cumbersome to be a serious challenge to the wired standard, but recent advances have given them quite a boost. Many cutting-edge companies have begun to switch to wireless networks, so you should definitely consider making the same move. Chapter 3 can help you decide both whether and when you should cut the networking cord.

Chapter 2

The Mobile-Computing Difference

It's official: Technology is now moving too quickly for any-one but a scientist to keep up. People are still talking about the Internet revolution—which, as you know, has been going on for only about ten years—yet the Internet no longer qualifies as the ultimate in technology. We have already begun to run across such phrases as "traditional wired Web" or the "old way of doing" something on a lap-top computer. You'd think they were talking about the pre-industrial era; it's almost unsettling to think that these phrases refer to a technology that has been popular for less than ten years.

And yet the terms are strangely appropriate. Technological progress is increasing exponentially. Rather than plugging along at a constant rate, it moves faster as the years—the months—pass by. The now famous Moore's Law, first proposed by Gordon Moore more than twenty-five years ago, predicted that microchip power would *double* every eighteen months. Many excellent scientists and engineers laughed. The years have proven Moore correct, except that he actually *underestimated* a bit. During the past decade, chip power increased at a faster pace than even Moore predicted. With progress moving at such a breakneck speed, then, it's understandable how technology can become outdated within a few years.

Thus the difficulty in publishing a computer book. No matter how up-to-date the developments are when the author writes about them, a few months can mean the difference between "cutting edge" and "last year's model." This book acknowledges such difficulties and tries to focus mostly on the more stable aspects of mobile computing: how the technology works, what general trends are developing, how businesses can best take advantage of mobility. Some aspects of mobile computing can be counted on.

Nevertheless, to stay on the safe side, we'll stick with the present and the immediate future. In all of the following situations, even though several are discussed in the future tense, the technology will be available quite soon, within the next few years. Many of even the most futuristic-sounding devices are already in use, though perhaps in a limited sense. We start by examining the vast benefits the world can expect from mobile computers in the next few years.

The Cool Stuff

Mobile computing is often thought of as an extension of wired computing. It's far more than that. It opens up entirely new avenues of productivity and will revolutionize customer service, advertising, and workplace efficiency. It will transform almost every industry, including the medical, educational, real estate, and construction fields. Once mobile truly grabs hold, the business world will never be the same.

> Mobile computing is often thought of as an extension of wired computing. It's far more than that.

But, perhaps most important, it has the potential to utterly shred the ties that shackle people to desks and home terminals, to change the way we work and interact with one another. One of the most pervasive stereotypes of the past ten years has been the socially isolated computer junkie, addicted to his PC screen. This can change. While wired computing requires one to be indoors, hidden away in either an office or home, wireless devices will allow people to stay connected—not just to the Internet, but to the outside world.

Just like your mom said to you during childhood: "It's a beautiful day. Go outside and play."

True Mobility

The most obvious benefit that mobile computing offers is, well, mobility. The Internet links us to people all over the world, but the wired Web cannot offer universal mobility. With wired technology, you may often find it difficult to keep in touch while on the move, on vacation, or simply away from your home office or PC. You're also unable to access important information without jumping through a complex series of hoops. Unfortunately, as time passes, frequent contact becomes more and more important. Telecommuting, conference calls, e-mail—all of these activities are no longer an option for many business people. Business has begun to shift from a focus on manufactured goods to an emphasis on data. Information itself is one of our hottest commodities, but it's also constantly changing, profoundly fluid. Society is on the move, and the public must run to keep up.

Cellular phones help to some extent, but they do not offer a complete solution. Traveling especially presents a number of problems. Forget to check your e-mail before you left your house? Oops. You'd better hope you can find a phone jack relatively soon, and that's if you're lucky enough to have a laptop computer. Do you need to fax that updated Excel sheet while at the airport? Uh, you'll have to wait. Want to doublecheck the weather at your destination? Maybe the pilot will mention it . . . maybe. And what's going on with those stocks you were interested in?

Mobile computing—especially the wireless Web— can solve these problems. It offers the busy, mobile public a way to stay truly connected. The Internet used to be a fantastic resource for at work and home. Now it's available anytime, anywhere.

Instant Information

The Internet is widely touted as being our most flexible, up-to-date method of communicating. This is completely true—it's currently the world's most direct source of knowledge. Mobile computing, with its wireless access to the Web, takes that advantage a giant step forward. The very mobility we just discussed also enables the user to receive up-to-date information, the minute she wants it.

If you have a bid placed on an eBay item, a Web-enabled phone can inform you instantly when someone has topped your offer. Your PC can't tell you immediately, especially if you're not at home; a special ring on your cell phone can. If you're at a restaurant and decide to go to a movie, that Palm VII can help you access reviews of the film. You can even buy the tickets while waiting for your entrees to arrive! If you're lost in a strange city and late for a meeting, your home PC cannot help you; but if you can download some maps to your smartphone, you're on your way. Stocks are especially known for their volatility—but, again, wireless technology enables you to stay on top of business, the second that it changes. College campuses are particularly excited about wireless potential, especially with the rising numbers of laptop-toting students. A couple campuses have even installed LAN receivers in some classrooms. Students with wireless-enabled laptops can access the Internet or share information with one another while still in the classroom.

Mobile computers help you *now*; you don't have to wait anymore. Information is power, but instant information is even better.

Personalization

The Internet is famous for its high level of personalization. This is a fair assessment on most levels; the Web does offer a measure of custom service unmatched by most brick-and-mortar companies. A user can design products online to match his specifications. Cookies— memory files planted by Web sites on the PC owner's hard drive—keep a record of the customer's history so that the company can offer deals or discounts tailored to that person's particular needs. A number of other services also combine to make the wired Internet a fine vehicle for individual attention.

The wireless Web, however, offers an even greater degree of personalization. Desktop computers are often used by more than one person—an entire family, perhaps, or roommates who share one PC. Mobile computers, on the other hand, are much more personal devices. PDAs and cell phones are almost always owned by one particular individual, who also happens to carry the item around on her person. Mobile phone numbers do not represent a family or household; they belong to an individual. The accompanying area code also pinpoints a person's exact location. Consumers stand to profit from information and advertising tailored specifically to their interests and needs.

Accordingly, mobile computers are a marketer's dream. With a simple ten-digit phone number, they'll be able to target sales to a very particular demographic, even down to the square block in which the person lives. It decreases the waste of resources and, when used properly, can increase the rate of customer response to each campaign.

Better Customer Service

Even in the retail world, wireless technology can work wonders. If a customer goes to a grocery store with a smartphone, she will be provided with an instant list of electronic coupons, specifically tailored to her shopping habits. Such technology benefits both business and consumer—the business makes more sales, and the consumer secures a better price on products she truly desires. It's personalization to the max.

In addition, the bar code technology utilized by businesses for internal management is also becoming useful to companies in the consumer capacity. Even now, some Web-enabled phones and PDAs are able to display electronic codes on their screens—and some savvy companies are taking advantage of the opportunity. Some airlines—most notably the Texas-based Aeritas—are experimenting with mobile, automated check-in services. A consumer registers for tickets over her phone, and the service then uses the voice patterns to establish a security check. The day of the flight, the traveler receives a call from the airport that offers final boarding and gate information; after the phone does a brief voice analysis to confirm her identity, a bar code appears on the face of the phone. Whenever she arrives at the airport, she can proceed directly to the gate, where the airline employees can scan her right in. Industry experts expect that such technology could become mainstream within one or two years.

Consumers hardly need be passive. Like corporate mobile scanners, a few PDAs and cell phones have built-in bar code scanners as well; consumers can now take an active role in improving their shopping experience. The added function has plenty of uses. Some companies use their specially equipped PDAs to order office supplies in a more efficient manner; the Office Depot system in particular is notable. The buyer takes the unit—in this case, the Quick Purchase Scanning PDA—to the local Office Depot and scans any item that she might be interested in ordering. The scan includes pricing, specifications, and other info that the buyer might need in making a product comparison. Once the device has the bar codes stored in its memory, the buyer takes it back to the office and downloads the product info onto the PC or the company common drive. Using special software that connects to the Office Depot Web site, the company can then place orders without going to the store. All the information is already at the buyer's fingertips; all she needs to do is check off the items that she wants—and because the bar codes are so accurate, there's no confusion at Office Depot about which products have been selected. The order can arrive the next day, without a bit of hassle.

> Like corporate mobile scanners, a few PDAs and cell
> phones have built-in bar code scanners as well;
> consumers can now take an active role in improving
> their shopping experience.

Bar code scanning capabilities will also soon be used for smarter consumer shopping. Suppose that Melissa goes shopping and finds a sweater that she likes; she tries it on and decides to buy it. In the past, she'd be forced to either pay the store's price or waste time scouring the city for a better bargain. Mobile computing changes everything.

Special Web sites will soon act as cross-brand product resources; they'll provide unbiased product reviews, price comparisons, and other relevant information. A shopper can simply scan a certain UPC into her PDA, then surf the Web site for a better deal. So Melissa can now— in one instant—find that exact same sweater for a bargain-basement price; she can then just go home and order it online. And she knows in advance that it will fit. Now *that's* a bargain!

Stores obviously won't be too thrilled about a new wave of PDA-wielding shoppers. In fact, the process might even be self-defeating. Retailers don't want their inventory to be used only for looking—they need people to buy items, as well. Stores that can't make any more sales will fold, which in turn will kill the shopper's ability to see products in person before making a purchase. Thus, what will happen in the event that PDA scanners become common is anyone's guess. Perhaps stores might ban handheld scanners, or the government might impose regulations on Web sites that provide bar code information; in any event, it's too soon to tell.

See Chapter 6 for more customer service ideas.

Easier Cashless Transactions

In Finland today, a hungry pedestrian can buy a candy bar with his cell phone. He simply checks the selection in the vending machine, makes a choice, and punches the corresponding numbers into his phone. The machine then produces the snack and adds the price of the purchase to the man's monthly phone bill. Grocery stores are also looking to install technology that can immediately bill a customer for his groceries—while his phone or debit card is still in a coat pocket! Indeed, as the years pass, fewer and fewer people will be inconvenienced by a lack of cash.

> In Finland today, a hungry pedestrian can buy a candy bar with his cell phone.

Emergency Medicine

Scientists are currently working on wireless devices that they can use on patients with serious chronic conditions. The computers will be programmed with the patient's medical information, along with any biological danger signals. Doctors could, for example, outfit an outpatient with a heart monitor—which could immediately page the hospital or 911 if the patient suffered a heart attack or other serious health problem. Not only would such wireless computers be able to notify emergency services, but they would also be able to transmit the patient's vital signs and allow medical technicians to arrive on the scene fully prepared for the situation.

Hospitals, too, are eager get their hands on mobile computers. Preliminary tests in a few locations around the country have proved wildly successful. Patient registration, which used to be a giant hassle, can now be performed right at a patient's bedside; the information is then transferred wirelessly to the general database for processing. Medical professionals are also looking forward to automatic medicine dispensation, which could be performed and logged in a similar fashion.

Greater Economy

Mobile phones and PDAs are far more budget-friendly than PCs. Although they can hardly be described as cheap, even the high-end, expensive models run to only a fraction of any desktop price. Lower prices are especially important given the life expectancy of a standard computer. In the current market, PCs are outdated in only two years! The short window of time forces the user to make a frequent and unpleasant choice: Either cope with a outdated unit or shell out more than $1,000 for a new one. It's not exactly a happy situation.

With a mobile unit, however, the consumer is in a far better position. In the first place, the computers themselves cost less. If you have to buy a new computer, it's better to spend a few hundred dollars than two thousand! Even better, though, many mobile phone companies have generous trade-in policies. Some companies allow customers to exchange old phones for new ones—absolutely free of charge. Now *that's* greater economy!

So why is price such a big deal? It enables a faster rate of market penetration. The public can more easily buy a mobile phone than a computer, which in turn increases the speed at which mobile computers are embraced by society. In Europe and Japan, where there's a very wide gap between wired and wireless costs, mobile technology is spreading like wildfire. The United States won't be far behind. And that's just the beginning. As the technology improves, people will be better able to continually upgrade their mobile unit, and at a minimal cost. Mobile computing is thus not only cheaper upon purchase; it's cheaper in the long run, as well.

Streamlined Infrastructure

Mobile computers aren't just good for customers; they can also revolutionize business from the inside. In addition to their obvious ability to improve internal communications, the new wave of devices will have a huge impact on data management. Many companies have employees who work in the field; in one study, about 60 percent of surveyed workers said that they operate outside their office. With employees in such far-flung locations, it can be incredibly difficult to maintain accurate, real-time internal data. Prices, stock levels, and important financial information fluctuate constantly. Although in-house employees have 24/7 access to the wired Intranet, field employees are often left with old data and "best guesses." Web-enabled PDAs or cell phones can let any employee tap into the database at any time and thus retrieve up-to-the-minute information. They will greatly improve employees' ability to make quick, appropriate decisions, no matter where they are.

> Mobile computers aren't just good for customers; they can also revolutionize business from the inside.

Along the same lines, some specialized mobile systems have for the past few years helped companies keep track of inventory. Warehouses and large stores use specialized wireless devices to scan bar codes and maintain a real-time, accurate inventory. The handheld units are all connected to a single LAN, which maintains a central database. As soon as the product is scanned, the item is entered into the computer; this information is thus immediately available to anyone else who has access to the database. This is a true boon to business. The method is efficient and painless and eliminates the mountains of paperwork and expensive hours of labor that used to accompany frequent hand inventory counts; it also makes better accuracy and product control. All of these qualities help the business cut costs, which more than makes up for the expensive handheld units. As time passes and prices fall, smaller companies will be more able to take advantage of such opportunities. Manual inventories will become a thing of the past.

See Chapter 3 for more information about wireless networks.

Drawbacks

When confronted by such a rosy picture of wireless technology, some might wonder why so few people have fully embraced it. According to an Accenture study published in March 2001, only 15 percent of international mobile device owners use their device to access the Web. Only about 1 percent have actually made a wireless purchase. It seems inexplicable. After all, wireless tech presents fabulous opportunities for both businesses and individuals—it is, without a doubt, the next revolution.

Yet, we must be realistic as well. Although mobile computing has undeniable potential, the fact remains that right now much about the new devices can't compete with established wired technology. The advances discussed in the preceding section are still in development; they're either brand-new or they haven't even come to the general market yet. For the present, mobile computing suffers from notable problems, just as most other innovations do. In this section we discuss a few of the most significant drawbacks.

Memory/Capacity

One of the biggest disadvantages of mobile devices is limited memory. While the average desktop PC can be expected to hold at least 80GB on its hard drive, wireless devices must make do with far less. Even high-quality laptop computers have just 20GB hard drives; this is fine for most users on the go, but it's still just 25 percent below the capacity of a regular computer. With a laptop, you must keep a strict rein on your downloading habits. PDAs are far more limited. They have only around 10 to 30MB of space, which is a mere fraction of desktop capacity. And mobile phone capacity is even more paltry—the best Web-enabled models still have less than 8MB.

Disk space is not the only deciding factor when someone is choosing a computer, but it certainly affects users' decisions about which machine to buy. Many people are still unwilling to own more than one computer, so they naturally opt for one that can fulfill many different roles; this in turn necessitates a unit with serious capacity, which usually means purchasing a PC. It's true that times are slowly changing as technology progresses. In the early days of mobile tech, almost all laptop owners were using them as secondary computers; laptops were not yet advanced enough to fulfill everyday needs. This is no longer the case. Laptop hardware has vastly improved over the past few years, and today some people are content to make their laptop their sole computer.

Yet, even now, most people opt for the power and storage space of a full-size PC unit; laptops are still mainly seen as backup. PDAs and Web-enabled cell phones, naturally, are virtually *always* used as satellites—they're intended to accompany the PC, not replace it. They're incapable of storing the vast array of programs and files necessary to the average user. And, until mobile computers can handle far more data, they will remain in the shadow of wired technology. If people can only buy *one* computer, they're not going to buy a PDA. Yet.

Limited Functionality

Mobile computers, excluding laptops, are also less functional. Their very mobility—their most salient advantage—is necessarily accompanied by reduced dimensions. After all, it's clearly impossible to be both portable *and* large! Unfortunately, the size is also a serious weakness. Cell phones and PDAs are too small to have full-size keyboards, which means that typing in information is still out of the question.

PDA manufacturers have come up with a few alternatives in data entry, but both are still inferior to the real thing: Miniature keyboards are awkward to use, and graffiti handwriting is both slower and less accurate than typing. Cell phones are even worse; most allow for data entry mainly through menu selection, where the user scrolls down a list and clicks on the desired option. Entering text is also a huge pain; each number represents at least three letters, so the user needs to enter two or three keystrokes just for one character. The data entry problem will probably be solved as time passes (see discussion later in this chapter), but there remains another problem: screen size.

A small screen size obviously limits the amount of material that the user can view on the handheld device. While the standard PC screen has a diagonal length of more than twelve inches, PDA displays generally are around three inches in area; cell phones screens, of course, are even tinier. Because of this inherent restriction, users simply cannot operate most applications the way they would on a regular desktop computer. The Web experience is also greatly hindered by the small screen size and inferior display quality—you usually won't see someone spend several hours surfing the Internet over her Nokia phone. Regardless of whether or not tech advances ever negate the data entry stumbling block, small displays are positively unavoidable. If you expand the screen to PC-size, suddenly your unit is no longer handheld. Size will thus probably condemn mobile computers to a permanently limited role in the user's life.

Low-Quality Connectivity

Consumers are undeniably demanding with regard to technology. They want the desired information to download as quickly as possible; delays are met with frustration and irritability. In a society where up-to-the-minute data are a precious commodity, time is at a very high premium. Handheld devices, then, have a notable drawback in that the embryonic technology is still a bit rough around the edges. Wireless connections are both slower and less reliable than those of wired devices, a fact that prevents users from fully embracing handhelds. Cutting-edge consumers are willing to use that PDA or Web-enabled phone when there's no other option, but it's not their first choice. The low-quality connectivity is caused by two main characteristics of mobile communication:

- **Bandwidth.** As discussed previously, wired modems are still the fastest way to travel the Web. Most of today's mobile units currently offer data transfer rates of only about one-fourth the speed of a standard 56K connection. People are notoriously impatient—especially now that they're accustomed to the brisk wired pace—so this leaves many handheld users cold. If you have a powerful home or office modem, you're more likely to confine your Web access to the desktop PC—it has more memory and a larger display, and it's faster, as well.

- **Coverage.** In America, at least, wired Web access and e-mail are far easier to procure; all the user need do is set up the software. The program then offers him a number of toll-free local access numbers. Less than two minutes later, he's online. It doesn't matter if he lives in Los Angeles or Weed Patch, California—there's always a phone number, always easy access.

  Wireless communication, on the other hand, is still far from a universal service. Although the European and Asian networks are almost all digital by now, American telecommunications are mostly analog—which, as we explained in Chapter 1, cannot host data transfer. Online services here are thus confined to a handful of well-populated metropolitan areas. Weed Patch is out of luck, and so are the travelers passing through the area. Because consumers know that their handheld device may very well fail to connect outside a major urban area, they are leery of relying too heavily on their mobile computers.

Limited Content

Web pages designed for desktop computers are not necessarily useful to people using a mobile device. In fact, mobile display screen sizes and resolutions are so different that programmers must frequently create a separate page intended specifically for handheld viewing if they want the Web page to be properly displayed by a wireless unit. (See Chapter 4.) Unfortunately, there's not yet an obviously compelling reason for online companies to develop special wireless pages. Remember that the numbers of wireless Web subscribers is still small, especially here in the United States. Most companies thus aren't willing to put in the time and resources to cater to such a tiny fraction of the populace; they don't see such an effort as worth the expected tiny Return on Investment (ROI).

Because there's a marked dearth of wireless Web content, then, wireless surfers are pretty much restricted to a limited pool of information and services. In their view, the very limited material cannot compete with the unlimited resources available on the traditional Internet—especially since they have to *pay* for access to that material. The result? Consumers are less likely to purchase a mobile computer in the first place. Which keeps the number of wireless subscribers small, which continues to limit content development. It's a regrettable but undeniable circle.

Expense

Finally, we can't fail to mention price. Paradoxically, mobile computers are both cheap and expensive. We discussed earlier in this chapter how they can be seen as a better bargain; they cost less than PCs and are easier to upgrade. But those benefits are mainly oriented toward future expenses; there are a few other factors to consider. The latest Web-enabled cell phones run from about $400 to $600 per unit. Although that's cheaper than any PC, it's not that great a bargain when you factor in the limitations we just discussed. In other words, many people would rather spend more money on a faster and more powerful product.

PDAs, which have been out for a bit longer, have proven the natural tendency of technology to grow cheaper as it becomes more established. Nevertheless, even the older, mediocre PDAs still cost at least $200 to $300. For that price, you don't even get the wireless Internet access. Want a Palm VII? You'd better be willing to hand over as much money as for a high-end Web phone. Bummer. The benefits of inexpensive mobile computers will outweigh PCs in the near future, but for many people, they haven't yet reached that point.

Finally, Europe is far more likely to embrace mobile technology first. American wireless consumers are patently conscious of those per-minute charges for mobile services. At home, they need pay only a flat fee for unlimited Internet access—if they're willing to put up with extra advertising, they might even get *free* unlimited access. On-location Web surfing doesn't appear as attractive when you have perfectly functional, inexpensive wired access at home.

The Silver Lining

Regardless of how serious the drawbacks described may appear, they should be taken in stride. All technology is weakest in its embryonic form. Scientists are dogged in their pursuits; they try, fail, learn, and try again. Each time they make an effort, they're a bit more successful. As time passes, the technology grows and matures; as it realizes its potential, the strengths gradually begin to overpower the limitations. Mobile computers still have some major kinks to work out, but it's only a matter of time before they come into their own. As you'll see in this discussion, most of the current problems will diminish or disappear over the next few years. In fact, in most cases, matters will have improved even by the time this book goes to press!

> Mobile computers still have some major kinks to work out, but it's only a matter of time before they come into their own.

Capacity

Resourceful programmers have already begun to find ways to enhance the memory space on handheld hard drives. As mentioned previously, for the past several years, technology has been comfortably outpacing Moore's Law. Advances follow so quickly upon one another's heels that it's difficult even for the experts to keep up. This is another reason why, of course, so many tech books seem to focus on *future* developments—their authors know that the present becomes outdated within months, while the future becomes reality at a blinding pace. In the next few years, look for PDAs and Web phones with more compact, internal memory chips that can hold up to several gigabytes of data.

Until internal drives can match consumer's needs, however, researchers have developed makeshift solutions to the capacity problem. Almost all PDAs and some 3G phones are built with expansion slots. Users can then simply purchase external memory cards that can hold up to 1GB of extra space, which is about one hundred times the capacity of the built-in drive! Expansion cards add a certain amount of bulk to the handheld device, but many users are content with the trade-off. Such cards allow individuals to really enhance the capability of their PDA; they're able to download far more PC-type programs; store music, pictures, or multimedia presentations; or simply carry more of their personal information around at their fingertips.

Data Transfer Rates

Data transfer rates, which currently support only about 14.4Kbps for handheld devices, will increase dramatically within a year or two. Already, technology is in place that will allow for speeds of at least the standard 56Kbps, and some networks are promising dedicated access and increased bandwidth to the tune of 300Kbps—which will rival DSL and other high-end wired access rates. And that's only for the 2.5 phones now appearing on the market. 3G models will be even faster!

Thanks to packet-switching and a variety of innovations, wireless systems are—as we mentioned before—in a constant upgrade process. Some companies are even choosing to skip the 2.5G stage, simply because they know that it won't last longer than a year or two. Why spend tons of money to upgrade your systems when you'll need to upgrade the upgrade so quickly? Instead, such companies have focused on moving directly from 2G to 3G service. Only a few large corporations are well financed enough to pay for that intermediate 2.5G stage; they want to keep their large public profile and thus are willing to pay extra to maintain their high-tech image.

Nevertheless, everyone will eventually upgrade—and sooner than you might think possible. Regardless of which exact path companies choose to take, technology always moves forward. Slow mobile connections, which present such a huge stumbling block to handheld Web and e-mail access, will disappear within a few short years.

Coverage

Although wireless services are still limited to an extremely few specific areas, they're slowly spreading. Cell phones and PDAs will soon benefit from wider digital coverage in the telecommunications industry. Within a few years, wireless Web support should be almost as comprehensive as standard cellular coverage.

Laptops with WLAN capabilities will also find support in an increasing number of places. A few airports already have wireless ports in their VIP lounges, and many more are likely to add the service within a few months or years. Companies such as MobileStar and Wayport provide the service, which is not limited only to airports. Some high-end resorts and hotels are choosing to install ports of their own, which enable travelers to wirelessly surf the Internet. Even Starbucks—yes, the coffee company—is looking into WLANs as well. In 2001, the company announced that it would try to have wireless access in 70 percent of its stores within two years. In any of these situations, all the laptop owner needs is the correct PC card.

Improved Functionality

Mobile computers are currently hindered by small screens, clumsy keys, and poor font resolution. Nevertheless, these drawbacks are becoming less of an obstacle with each passing month. Manufacturers are supremely conscious of mobile design limitations and are working feverishly to minimize them.

As time passes, phone screens are growing ever larger—even at the expense of overall size. This trend attests to the future importance of mobile Internet access. In the past few years, cell phones have grown smaller and smaller. Now, rather than solely focusing on a reduction in the overall profile of the device, companies are choosing to throw their assets behind the wireless Web.

Just look at any of the most recent WAP offerings: Some of the handsets are almost all screen. A few models allow for the increased area by designing a flip keypad, which is normally positioned over the bottom half of the handset. When the user wants to surf the Internet, she needs only to unhook the keypad and flip it down, thus revealing more of the display. Other manufacturers have created phones with touch screens. The keys are represented only on the display—they can be pressed like regular key buttons, but they can also disappear when not in use, thus freeing up more valuable screen space. Roller bars and arrow keys also increase functionality without taking up too much room.

Finally, one company in particular has developed software that makes entering text much easier. While most current text entry requires the user to hit a key as many as three or four times before selecting a single letter, Tegic's T9-enabled phones reduce the hassle by leaps and bounds. All the user need do is hit each key once per character, choosing the number that contains the desired letter. When the entry is completed, the program then suggests the most likely word given that particular combination of numbers. T9 is incredibly popular and has been licensed to about 90 percent of the mobile phone market.

Still, none of these solutions is ideal. Entering words and other information is still tricky, and researchers are toiling to produce the only true solution: voice recognition.

Voice Recognition

The difficulty of data entry, one of the greatest mobile stumbling blocks, may soon be solved by the development of voice recognition programming. Scientists have been feverishly working to produce a practical Voice Enabled Interface (VEI), a system that will allow the user to enter commands and surf the Internet without having to fumble with a stylus or numerical keypad. A good VEI would be of incalculable importance to the mobile computing industry. Consumers often use their handheld devices on the move, which, after all, is the whole point of going mobile. In such situations, they're usually juggling at least two different activities: They're clicking or entering data with only one hand, while driving, carrying a briefcase, opening doors, or accomplishing other mundane tasks at the same time. Such situations make for laborious handheld use. Voice recognition would go a long way toward simplifying wireless use.

Primitive VEIs have been available to wired PC owners for the past few years; users can open and close files, dictate word documents, and accomplish other tasks simply by speaking to the computer. Admittedly, existing VEI systems still have plenty of bugs to work out; even the best programs have only about 90 percent accuracy. This might sound like a pretty good percentage, until you consider that the computer will screw up at least once every ten to fifteen words. It's a bigger problem than you might think. When you're typing on a keyboard, it's easy to fix a typo—just backspace and correct the error. With a VEI, however, backing up is a lot more complicated.

Wireless VEIs have one more main obstacle to overcome before they can be truly practical: storage. VEI programs take up a lot of hard disk space; right now, they're simply too cumbersome to install on wireless units. Even on comparatively spacious desktop PCs, VEI programs take up a huge percentage of the hard drive; mobile units wouldn't even be able to carry a fraction of the software necessary to run the application.

Engineers are aware of this problem and are working on a solution. Although mobile computers may be incapable of storing VEI locally (that is, within their own memory banks) for the foreseeable future, they are far more able to host a real-time connection with voice software stored on a separate server. Such situations are sometimes referred to as "thin-client," because the client (mobile unit) is able to access a large cache of applications without needing to bulk up its own memory banks. Because the enabling structure at least is already in existence, scientists predict that they'll be able to produce a working, thin-client VEI model within the next few years.

The most likely vehicle for such an application is VoiceXML, a text-based language that is able to transmit programs for voice services over the airwaves, just like HTML, Java, and other traditional programming languages. Chapter 4 describes VoiceXML in more detail.

Broader Content

For all of the reasons discussed in this chapter, handheld computers will gradually become more functional. In turn, more people will purchase units, and the wired Web will grow increasingly popular. This is exactly the boost that content developers need to justify giving the wireless Web the serious attention that it deserves. Within the next couple of years, expect the amount of wireless content on the Internet to grow exponentially.

This effect, interestingly, will become a cause. The increasingly rich material and utility of the wireless Web itself will make mobile units more attractive purchases— which will encourage more people to buy one and to subscribe to an access service.

Chapter 3

Internal Affairs—WLANs

Wireless networking technology has been around for several years, but businesses have been slow to embrace it. It's hardly surprising. No matter how easy it is to set up and run a wireless network, speed far outweighs convenience in nearly all internal business tasks and communication. Unfortunately, for a long time, wireless networks were too sluggish for most companies to consider trying them out; WLANs first matched the old, wired 1974 Ethernet 10Mbps speed only a couple of years ago. Yet, though wireless networks got a relatively slow start, they're now finally beginning to gain some momentum. Faster processing and new standards have become widely available;

The tide is turning—many companies now see wireless networks as an attractive option.

even though WLANs haven't yet reached wired speeds, they're getting fast enough to be practical. The tide is turning—many companies now see wireless networks as an attractive option.

Benefits of WLANs

WLANs are different from most of the other wireless technologies described in this book. While cell phones, PDAs, and pagers are highly mobile, portable items, WLANs are deployed to connect more stationary devices, usually laptops or PCs. (Bluetooth is a notable exception and is discussed at length later in this chapter.) Also, rather than using the cellular communications system, WLANs allow the computers to interact directly with one another. WLANs can be used in a wide variety of situations, all of which benefit from the wireless advantage.

- **Simplicity.** Setting up a traditional local-area network involves a veritable Gordian tangle of wires and cables. The process takes hours—perhaps days—as IT workers sort out the lines of communication. Wired LANs can force employers to run wires around rooms, under furniture, or even through thick walls. Businesses that operate in older facilities can face even greater challenges.

  WLANs, on the other hand, can be implemented

in a fraction of the time. All it takes is a few wireless access points and limited set-up on the member devices.

- **Fluidity.** Ethernet LANs are rigid in structure. The wires physically bind the computers to one another, making any changes to the system difficult. If a new employee starts at a company, providing her with a wired terminal is a huge pain. Someone has to run cables to the new cubicle, which may or may not be in an easily accessible spot. Switching workstations is equally tricky.

    WLANs are fluid—that is, they're extremely flexible. All any new employee needs is a network-compatible terminal and proximity to a wireless access point. That's it. If other workers need to rotate cubicles or move to a different office, all they have to do is move the computer. The WLAN moves right with them.

    Wireless flexibility is also helpful in temporary situations. Business professionals at a convention or meeting are able to set up in a matter of minutes, leave the network in place for the day, then easily strike it when the convention ends.

    > Wireless flexibility is also helpful in temporary situations.

- **Added mobility.** Finally, WLANs do create a greater degree of mobility. Granted, WLANs cannot transmit a signal thousands of miles, as cell phones can; after all, they *are* supposed to be local. Nevertheless, they allow business travelers and field employees to maintain a connection even when roaming about.

For example, a warehouse might set up access points throughout the building, allowing employees with handheld devices to maintain accurate, real-time inventory counts. The executives—perhaps in a meeting upstairs—could be wirelessly linked to the company database and would also have immediate access to this data. WLANs, properly installed, have the potential to eliminate nearly all information latency.

As mentioned in Chapter 2, business travelers can take advantage of wireless access points in airports and hotels; the only drawback is that these are public networks and thus grant only access to the World Wide Web, not to the company network. These situations, therefore, cannot be categorized as internal networks. Still, such capabilities are very useful.

Disadvantages of WLANs

Despite the WLANs' undeniably bright future, they're not perfect. Given their relatively recent appearance and the youth of the technology, developers are still working to minimize various problems. It's important for managers to consider the drawbacks before they take any action; they can then make a balanced decision.

- **Speed.** Here is the most obvious factor. WLANs, as mentioned previously, currently support only a fraction of wired data speeds. This is improving, most notably with the 802.11a standard (discussed later in this chapter), but WLANs will be significantly slower for years to come. Any company that places a premium on speed should consider whether the business would be adversely affected by a poky WLAN.

- **Power.** WLANs are also limited by physical distances. Since wirelessly networked computers must communicate directly with an access point, they need to be in close proximity in order for the system to function properly. Maximum ranges for the most recent products run from about 100 to 500 feet indoors to more than 1,500 feet outdoors. The indoor range is greater because it allows for a clear line of sight; the more walls and other obstacles between the access point and the terminal, the shorter the range. In addition, the data transfer slows as the distance approaches the maximum range.

- **Security.** Security is probably the most salient wireless concern. In a wired network, outside access is impossible without a physical link to the system. Security is thus fairly tight; the danger exists mainly from hackers who might try to break into the system.

  With WLANs, however, the data are being transmitted over the open airwaves, which lack clear structure. After all, nobody can make a radio signal respect such arbitrary boundaries as a door or wall. An access point provides an entry point to the system for anyone who happens to be close enough: the secretary in the office suite next door, the engineer across the street— or even the hacker in the basement. Early WLAN users were either ignorant of the dangers or stuck trying to control access to an intangible signal. They didn't always succeed. There are many instances in which an outside party accidentally gained access to a WLAN Intranet. Such a situation makes for poor security, which in turn is a huge problem.

Since no one can yet divert or control signals, the only real way to safeguard sensitive information is to transmit in code. Many tech companies are thus working feverishly to create high-quality encryption software. We discuss this more in-depth later on in the chapter.

Wireless Standards

Despite the obvious drawbacks of wireless networks, the advantages are solid enough that more and more companies are choosing to make the switch from Ethernet to WLAN. It's important, then, to survey the playing field. What's out there?

Quite a lot, actually. Because the technology has advanced so rapidly, no one standard has become universal. By the time any version gains a foothold, it seems, a tech company debuts an even faster standard. There is thus a wide variety of existing WLANs, all of which vary in quality. In order to make the wisest decision, any business that considers implementing wireless a network should be able to distinguish among the main wireless standards.

In order to make the wisest decision, any business that considers implementing wireless a network should be able to distinguish among the main wireless standards.

• **HomeRF.** The HomeRF (Home Radio Frequency) standard was one of the first wireless networking protocols; it was developed by the HomeRF Working Group, an industry alliance with a few powerful players. Although it got off to a great start, with a low retail price and backing from Intel and Proxim, it was hampered by a slow 1.6Mbps data rate. By the time it began working on modifications that would allow speeds from 11Mbps, faster competitors had already left HomeRF behind. Although some big, early corporate adopters still use HomeRF—not including Intel, which abandoned ship—you'd do better to consider its diminishing stature. If you're thinking about going wireless, don't use the Home RF standard.

• **IEEE 802.11.** IEEE stands for Institute of Electrical and Electronic Engineers. (Don't worry about the numbers—just be able to recognize the system to which they refer.) 802.11 was the earliest wireless standard; it was implemented in the 1990s along with a number of other competitors, but it quickly emerged as the most prominent choice. Incidentally, the IEEE folks are the ones who developed the Ethernet, so the coattail effect is probably one good reason that it enjoyed an early advantage.

802.11 first transmitted its data via the FHSS

method, with the signal hops occurring almost eighty times per second. Although the technology worked, it still had some serious weaknesses. The data transfer rate was incredibly sluggish by wired network standards—approximately 1.6Mbps. In addition, if any information is blocked, the system has to resend one of the data packets. Because FHSS was a tad unreliable, then, many 802.11 systems began to use DSSS technology. With the massive DSSS broadcasts, data are more likely to arrive intact; they can also be transmitted more quickly, at about twice the speed of the FSSS version. Because of its success, the DSSS version of 802.11 soon became the stepping stone to the next generation of wireless network technology.

• **IEEE 802.11b.** 802.11b looks to be the most popular standard—by far—for the next few years. It's based on the DSSS method, like 802.11; the difference is simply that it's more advanced. (Those engineers never stop to rest, do they?) First and foremost, IEEE 802.11b is capable of data speeds up to 11Mbps, which just surpassed the original wired standard.

It also offers a higher degree of data integrity. 802.11b is based on the CSMA/CA, or Carrier Sense Multiple Access Collision Avoidance protocol. What that long string of words means is that 802.11b communication ensures that all data are safely received. The transmitting node first ensures that the frequency is clear before sending a data packet. It then waits for the ack packet from the receiver; if it doesn't get the ack packet within a certain amount of time, it resends the data. In this way, little information is lost through the wireless transmission.

Such breakthroughs helped power the recent surge in the popularity of wireless networks. Few people in 2000 took advantage of wireless technology, even though it was easily obtainable. It took the increased speed of 802.11b for consumers to sit up and take notice—and now, suppliers can hardly keep up with demand.

The 802.11b standard is frequently referred to as the High Rate Standard. Manufacturers of devices that adhere to the standard are given the seal of approval by the Wireless Ethernet Compatibility Alliance (WECA). Their products are then referred to as Wi-Fi (Wireless Fidelity) compliant. All Wi-Fi devices, regardless of the brand type, are interoperable; they're able to "speak" to one another through the network.

- **IEEE 802.11a.** Practically before 802.11b makes it out of the gates, it's being confronted by yet another competing standard: 802.11a. Yes, "b" came before "a"; although they were developed at the same time, the 802.11a version was more complex and thus took longer to refine. Regardless of the speed with which it came to market, however, 802.11a is a significant improvement on the "b" version. It's still far from the multi-Gbps of wired networks, but 802.11a can support data transmission rates of nearly 54Mbps— that's almost one hundred times faster than the standard wired Internet access speed. Not bad. Notably, despite the similar name tags, 802.11a is not compatible with 802.11b. There are a few reasons, the most salient being that "a" transmits on an entirely different radio band. Neither does it use spread spectrum technology; instead, it employs Orthogonal Frequency Division Multiplexing (OFDM). OFDM helps minimize interference in wireless networks, and is undeniably an improved standard. But there are always a few hitches.

First, it's not yet widely available, although 802.11a went on limited sale in 2001. It also has a smaller broadcast range than Wi-Fi. The main problem is that it's more expensive than "b"—for the time being, anyhow. Since price is key to the popularity of any technological development, the Wi-Fi standard will probably dominate the network airwaves for the next few years. Wi-Fi has also had some time (no matter how brief) to establish itself. 802.11a, though technically superior, will start out fighting an uphill battle. Nobody quite knows what's going to happen, especially since even more 802.11 versions are expected to appear in the near future: 802.11g and 802.11e.

What all IEEE standards have in common, however, is that they are still unable to penetrate European markets. Overseas countries have their own pet standards: the HiperLan series.

- **HiperLan.** HiperLan is the brainchild of the European Telecommunications Standards Institute, the same group that produced GSM and other European radio systems. HiperLan, like the IEEE standards, has gone through several incarnations over the past several years. Right now, the most prevalent is HiperLan 2, which is backed by such high-profile corporations as Ericsson, Nokia, and Philips. HiperLan 2 actually uses the same OFDM technology as 802.11a, but they're not currently compatible; they're transmitted on different spectrums. Although HiperLan is most popular overseas, it's looking to establish itself as the global standard.

Which of these standards eventually becomes a global wireless networking standard remains to be seen. IEEE and HiperLan are the prime candidates for supremacy, but there's no guarantee that either will ever claim ultimate victory. As entrenched as they are in their respective locales, these two standards may actually wind up coexisting for a very long time. They may even learn to get along. The Atheros company has proposed a standard called 5-UP that would allow the competing standards to interoperate. There's just one more system that warrants discussion at this time: the famous Bluetooth standard.

Bluetooth

Bluetooth is a WLAN like the other networks we just explored, but there are a few major differences. Most important, Bluetooth is designed to work with all kinds of electronic devices, not just laptop and desktop computers. That includes PDAs, pagers, and cell phones, but it also includes household appliances, entertainment systems, headphones, and any other gadget that can be made compatible. Bluetooth thus signals an incredibly ambitious effort, which is probably the main reason that it has generated such a significant buzz.

Bluetooth is named for Harald Bluetooth, an ancient Viking king who united Denmark and Norway during the Middle Ages. The implication here is fairly obvious; Bluetooth technology was created for the same purpose: unification. Back in 1998, a group of telecommunications giants, including Ericsson, Nokia, Intel, Toshiba, and IBM, joined forces to create the Bluetooth Special Interests Group (SIG), a consortium with the stated goal of finding a way for mobile phones to communicate with other, previously unconnected electronic units. Eventually, the project grew in scope until it became a quest for a system to connect any electronic device to just about any other electronic device. The effort has certainly generated a great deal of derision since its inception; there have been numerous jokes about Internet toasters and "SmartRefrigerators."

Yet the sheer ingenuity—the vision—of the idea inspired enough people to help bring the idea to fruition. More than 2,000 companies eventually made serious investments in the technology, and the intense pressure helped bring Bluetooth to the market right on schedule. Bluetooth made its official debut early in 2000. Enter reality.

Very few Bluetooth-enabled products actually became available, and those that did encountered a lukewarm market; consumer demand was lackluster at best. Even the Bluetooth products that did make it to sale have mostly been external, expansion devices, not the tiny internal chips that had been promised. Then the endless debate set in. There's still plenty of talk about whether or not Bluetooth will survive. Some pundits just can't imagine that such a high degree of connectivity could be workable at the present time. So just how realistic *is* it?

How Bluetooth Works

It's probably best to first explain what Bluetooth technology actually entails. The actual Bluetooth chip works on the same frequency as Wi-Fi devices, but it uses different method of broadcasting. While Wi-Fi now uses DSSS, Bluetooth signals hop frequencies in the style of the original FHSS 802.11. If you thought that eighty jumps per second was fast, check out the Bluetooth rate: more than 1,500 *times per second*! Bluetooth chips are also tiny; they can be built in to just about any kind of electronic device, from widescreen TVs to wristwatches.

Bluetooth was largely conceived of as a way to replace the IR (infrared) technology of recent years. So far, IR has been the only way for mobile computers to wirelessly share information. Many PDAs are equipped with an IR port; if you line them up, you can beam data back and forth. Many consumers enjoyed the convenience of syncing their handhelds without having to bring along extra cables and adapters.

But IR technology fails to offer the universality of Bluetooth; it works from PDA to PDA, but none of the IR ports can turn on the TV or set the VCR clock. In addition, IR requires a direct line of sight in order to function, which isn't always feasible. Imagine using IR to send a captured Web page from your cell phone to your PDA while driving.

You'd have to hold both, carefully aligning the IR ports while trying to steer at the same time. That would be not only ridiculously difficult but highly dangerous and irresponsible, as well.

Bluetooth networks through groupings called piconets. Each piconet can support up to eight devices, all of which have a direct channel of communication with one another. Piconets can then interact to form larger scatternets. Even if devices on a scatternet cannot directly see one another, they can still interact, as long as they are close enough. The Bluetooth range is currently about thirty feet.

Once within range of one another, Bluetooth-enabled devices interact continuously, and in set patterns. Every device can be categorized as either active or passive. Active Bluetooth computers constantly search their environment, looking for other Bluetooth units. Passive units are, well, *passive*. They sit quietly in place and react only to an initiated conversation. They're like the traditional obedient child who speaks only when spoken to. Once an active unit finds another device, it initiates a brief conversation. It sends an electronic introduction that states its identity (PDA? Cell phone? Laptop?) and its capabilities. The other device then responds in kind. The active device is then called the "master," since it initiates the conversation.

After the devices have introduced themselves, the master device then decides whether it needs anything from the passive unit, which is now called the "slave." If it doesn't, then they simply remain aware of each other; if the master device eventually needs anything, then it transmits a pairing request. Here's where the slave unit has a chance to speak up; it has the right to deny a pairing if the master does not satisfy ID or security requirements. Both parties must be willing in order for a pairing to occur.

And what's the pairing? It's whatever task or exchange of information the master unit desires. It can send a request for a coffeemaker to brew coffee or to gain access to a PC database. All of this action must take place within the confines of a single piconet.

Each piconet has, in turn, only one master device and up to seven slave devices. But the arrangement is far from stifling: Any Bluetooth device is able to switch from one piconet to another at will. Let's see what's possible in a Bluetooth network.

Imagine that Susan comes to pick Dan up for a business trip, and they are sitting in his car in the driveway, about to leave. They both have PDAs and cell phones, and Dan also has a wireless headset and laptop computer with him—and, of course, every device contains the proper enabling chip. Dan can use his Web-enabled phone to download driving directions, then transfer them directly to his PDA, which has a larger screen and can better display maps. He and Susan then quickly check to make sure that their PDA appointment books are synced; they don't want to miss an important meeting. They're almost ready to go, but Dan wants some good driving music, so he has his PDA transmit his favorite MP3 files to the headset for while they're traveling. As they pull out of the driveway, Dan suddenly remembers that he left the TV on. He quickly uses his cell phone to shut it off. Bluetooth has the potential to radically streamline the way people interact with computers and other electronics. It's revolutionary.

The Bluetooth Reality

For all its promise, however, Bluetooth has gotten off to an undeniably slow start. After a full year in circulation, Bluetooth products are still mostly limited to a few external PDA extension cards and other adapters. No company has yet begun to mass-market products that have Bluetooth hardwired into the circuitry. Price is part of the reason; the chips still cost $10 to $15 each, and manufacturers are loath to add that into their retail price until there's significant demand for the capability. (The Bluetooth SIG hopes to lower the price to a supposed critical mass point of $5 within a year or two.) Besides price, experts cite shortcomings in the technology itself. They point to a number of apparent flaws as reasons that Bluetooth hasn't made the immediate splash everyone expected.

First, the Bluetooth throughput is lower than just about any other recent wireless network—it usually maxes out at around 800Kbps, rather than at the Mbps speeds most WLANs achieve. This prevents Bluetooth from being an attractive option for high-speed professional networking. But that's not necessarily all bad. The frequent jumps mean that it's very difficult to degrade a Bluetooth signal. Each packet transmitted on a certain frequency lasts only the barest microfraction of a second; if that packet is destroyed by interference, the signal is still mostly intact. Bluetooth is slower, but it is also stronger.

Yet even the low throughput is not too much of a problem. Bluetooth was not designed to replace traditional wired networking; it was created primarily to connect previously unconnected units. It's not specialized for laptop-laptop or PC–PC networks, although it does have that capability. Instead, it's for cell–PDA or PDA–headphones or cell–VCR exchanges. It's harder to complain about slow data transfer rates in these situations. They also simply don't require the same high capacity exchanges that PCs need. The needs of a cell phone are more modest.

The second distinguishing characteristic of Bluetooth is its shorter broadcast range. While standard WLANs can transmit signals up to three hundred feet away, Bluetooth is limited to about one-tenth that distance. The obvious point here is that the Bluetooth infrastructure is both more complicated and cumbersome; 802.11b networks need far fewer access points than do Bluetooth networks. Bluetooth signals just don't have the necessary power.

Again, however, there's a reason that Bluetooth ranges are so limited: A shorter range preserves precious battery life. The network was designed to run primarily on wireless portable devices; desktop PCs may have unrestricted access to electricity, but mobile computers must make do with whatever battery power they carry with them. The Wi-Fi signal's very power also saps the strength of every compliant unit within its radius. Bluetooth, on the other hand, presents far less of a strain. Quite simply, Bluetooth's unassuming nature is intentional. It was designed to keep a low profile.

To most experts, then, the current Bluetooth "slump" is temporary. Expectations had risen so high and entailed such unbelievable claims that the reality was bound to be a bit of a letdown. Bluetooth is a real technology and has real problems. Companies are now finally coming to terms with its limitations. But the reevaluation will also reinvigorate the campaign. Once consumers can see Bluetooth as more than a miraculous novelty, they will finally be able to fully embrace its undeniable real-world benefits. The first truly commercial Bluetooth products, with a built-in chip, will be made available in 2002. Companies such as SymbolTechnologies Inc. are betting on success. So are we. Despite the slow start, expect Bluetooth to be a major business player within five to ten years.

Deploying Your Own Wireless Network

WLANs are an efficient networking tool for many businesses, even the smaller ones. The companies that stand to benefit the most are those that find it impractical to implement an Ethernet version. Some lease space in a building that forbids drilling into walls or floors; this can make matters incredibly difficult if you have employees on different floors or in different suites. Other offices simply have a complicated layout, with all kinds of equipment and furniture standing in the intended cable path. It's true that WLANs are generally more expensive, but, in certain cases, the real-world costs of a wired network can outpace a simple wireless version.

Yet, even if your company can easily install the Ethernet, or even if it already has the network solidly in place, adding a wireless overlay might be a good idea. Adding a few wireless access points can allow for a far greater degree of office mobility and ensure that employees can access information from wirefree rooms, perhaps the conference room or lunch area. Either way, it's certainly worth thinking about.

Choosing a Standard

Once you know the relative merits of available WLAN standards, it's not too difficult to make a choice. Most small companies would be wise to go with the popular 802.11b protocol; it's the most universal standard available, so there are a lot of Wi-Fi compliant products on the market. Finding good hardware is thus an easy task, and you're ensured the highest possible degree of interoperability. Finally, 802.11b is fairly inexpensive.

> Once you know the relative merits of available WLAN standards, it's not too difficult to make a choice.

If the 10Mbps speed isn't fast enough for your company's purposes, then 802.11b isn't really ideal. That's why a few higher-end companies are deciding to use 802.11a. It's about five times faster than the older version, which lessens the penalty of going wireless. Nevertheless, 802.11a products have barely begun to appear on the market. They're also incompatible with Wi-Fi compliant units and cost a great deal more. For almost any small business, 802.11b is the way to go. The following advice is offered on the assumption that you're using Wi-Fi devices.

Getting Hardware

Once you've settled on a method of communication, you still need actual hardware. Not surprisingly, many companies find themselves paralyzed at this stage of the process. Since Wi-Fi-compliant circuitry is the most widely available, you'll have to select from myriad possible wireless ports and PC cards. Picking "just one" thus might seem nearly impossible. There's good news, however: Selecting hardware is not as difficult as you think.

Wireless Access Points

Wireless access points provide exactly what the name implies: access to the server and database. Despite the abundance of choices, most wireless access points are actually fairly generic. Advertisements and labels might claim otherwise, but almost all of them transmit at approximately the same rate out to the same distance: fifty feet. Yes, the maximum range is farther, but greater distance is achieved only at a sacrifice of speed. Almost any company would rather buy more access points and maintain the highest data-transfer rate possible.

The key considerations for smaller companies, then, are price, installation, and ease of troubleshooting. Price is listed for obvious reasons. As for the last two, they're most important if you don't have a full IT staff. After all, what good is a wireless network if you can't install it or fix it when something malfunctions?

A few of the best products: D-Link's Air Wireless, which is dirt-cheap and easy to install; AmbiCom's

Wave2Lan, which is also fairly inexpensive; LinkSys' Instant Wireless is more costly, but offers a good 128-bit encryption for more security-minded companies. All three options are of good quality and sell for under $250 in a market where access points can easily go for almost $400.

Wireless access points take care of half the WLAN—more specifically, the external half. They are the intermediaries, like the cellular towers of telecommunications; they create a wireless link to the server for any compliant device located within range. Still, computers cannot interface with the wireless access point unless they also have the proper hardware. Wireless networking capabilities are still rarely hardwired into PC or laptop circuitry and thus must be purchased separately. Such equipment usually takes the form of either special PC cards or USB adapters.

PC Cards

Virtually all modern laptops come with a PC card slot. Therefore, manufacturers have begun producing PC cards that add wireless capability to the unit; they usually have one or two antennas attached to the exterior part of the card, which send and receive the signals.

Such cards generally cost approximately $200 each and fit directly into the PC slot. Most versions of Windows, such as 98 or Me, automatically recognize this type of PC card and immediately display the proper installation prompts, making setup a breeze. 3Com's Air-Connect PC card is extremely popular, offering 128-bit encryption and easy setup; AmbiCom's Wave2Lan PC card is just as effective, however, and sells for far less. As with access points, quality is rarely a big factor; nearly all PC cards produced by reputable companies work equally well.

Unlike laptops, however, many PCs do not come with a PC card slot. Therefore, if you want to go the PC card route with a desktop computer, you might need a PC card adapter. Such devices are easily inserted into an empty drive slot, right where you'd normally place a floppy disk.

USB Ports/Adapters

When working with desktop PCs, USB adapters are often the best option. USB (Universal Serial Bus) ports come on virtually all desktop computers, negating the need for a special PC card adapter. Some companies use the USB port on their laptop as well, especially if there's a mix of laptops and desktops in their office. It minimizes the fuss of switching between one type and the other. D-Link's Air DWL-120 USB adapter is an excellent choice, as is Acer NeWeb's USB offering. Both are inexpensive, selling for only $100 or so.

Extras

Computers aren't the only units that can be roped into a wireless network. Other peripheral devices can be included as well, given the proper adapter. The most common are gateway routers and wireless print servers. Gateway routers can provide access to both the Internet and the wired Ethernet system—that is, if your office is wired for Ethernet. Print servers, such as D-Link Systems'

Air DP313 Wireless model, plug into printers and allow computers to print from the station without wires. As time passes, pretty much any piece of office equipment will be able to join the wireless network.

> If you're looking to secure your WLAN, you have a number of options.

WLAN Security

Remember that WLANs are vulnerable to hacking because they rely on radio signals to communicate. Since it's almost impossible to control sound waves, technicians have had to develop other ways to keep internal data safe from prying eyes. If you're looking to secure your WLAN, you have a number of options.

Network Encryption

Encryption is by far the most widespread and most reliable way to preserve the integrity of a wireless network. The most basic level of security offered by 802.11b adapters is 40-bit WEP, or Wired Equivalent Privacy. WEP technology encrypts each packet before it's sent. As you probably noticed, some systems offer 64- or even 128-bit encryption, but they're also more expensive. Small business managers and owners should consider carefully how sensitive their internal data are as they decide whether higher-bit encryption is worth the added price. Encryption also slows the network to a certain degree, because it has to encode and decode every data packet that's sent and received.

Regardless, be sure that your wireless access point doesn't have a lower-bit level than your PC card or USB adapters; the overall encryption can only be as high as the access point's level, so a 128-bit encryption PC card would be wasted in a system with 40-bit wireless access points. For a more lengthy discussion of wireless encryption, see Chapter 6.

SSID

SSID, or Service Set ID, is an application that requires users to have a special PC card installed in their notebooks, which in turn need to request the access point by name. This prevents casual bystanders or nearby eavesdroppers from easily or inadvertently being allowed into the network. SSID isn't perfect, however. Every card has the same SSID, which isn't exactly ideal. SSID works best with a second level of security; the PC card should also be equipped with a MAC address.

MAC

Media Access Control—or MAC—addresses are like the guest list at a fancy party. A programmer enters the wireless access point's management interface and enters the Ethernet addresses of all users who will be allowed to access the network. This beefs up security considerably. If an individual with an unauthorized SSID on a PC card tries to access the WLAN, he still won't have a valid MAC address on his card. He'll then be denied access.

In other words, it's like trying to crash the fancy party. No matter how much you beg, if you're not on the guest list, the doorman simply won't let you in. You can't just show up and join the action.

Passwords

Finally, we wouldn't want to forget the old standby: password protection. Many WLAN products come equipped with password protection software. That's always a bonus and adds one final layer of security.

But Is It Safe Enough?

All things considered, WLANs are safe enough to install in any ordinary company. Major companies wouldn't be making the switch to wireless networks if they felt that the systems were at all insecure. Although the available security measures are not completely foolproof, they'll more than suffice—that is, unless you're doing top-secret military research. But that's unlikely, isn't it?

All things considered, WLANs are safe enough to install in any ordinary company.

Putting It All Together

Now that you've purchased the hardware, it's time to actually deploy the network. Since the adapters and the access points are all generally easy to install, most of the work revolves around deciding both how *many* access points to buy and where to put them. If you have too few, then your data transfer rate will suffer. Of course, buying too many is not good either—it's a waste of money. Therefore, you'll have to plan carefully before you run out to buy access points; make sure you know how many you'll need.

Most 802.11b systems transmit reliably at maximum speed for about for about fifty to sixty feet (with an obstructed or clear line of sight) before the speed starts to suffer. If the devices are much farther apart than that, Wi-Fi equipment will begin to downgrade the transfer rate to accommodate the greater distance. If it can't achieve the ideal 11Mbps, then it will try at 5Mbps; failing that, it will try again at 1Mbps. If it can't process at that final rate, it will give up.

The good news is that the PC or laptop Wi-Fi nodes do some of the work for you. Wherever the computers are located, they'll seek out the strongest access point signal, then lock on. In other words, you don't have to worry about whether they'll find the optimum access point. It also doesn't matter how many terminals are paired with a single access point; a single access point can perform with any number of individual terminals. You will, however, need to make sure that there's at least one access point close enough to share a strong signal with every terminal.

When positioning wireless access points in your office, then, you should allow for no more than fifty feet between each workstation and access point. If two terminals are located one hundred feet apart, then you should place an access point directly in the middle. Each station would then be only fifty feet from an access point, and thus both would be able to operate at the full 11Mbps. For greater numbers of workstations, you'll probably need to play around with possible locations until you've optimized the overall placement: the fewest number of access points possible to ensure each terminal's fastest speed.

Chapter 4

Your Need for M-Commerce

Although mobile computers have numerous personal and corporate uses, the most notable innovation of mobile technology is the ability to receive Internet access from virtually anywhere. The number of Web-enabled hand-held devices is growing steadily, and the pace will only increase as the months pass. At some point, it will reach a critical mass of sorts—and it will burst upon the public consciousness as abruptly as the Internet did in 1995. Within the next couple of years, the wireless Web is suddenly going to be major commercial force.

Smart businesses everywhere should thus take note of the situation. "M-commerce" (mobile commerce) is like the

Oklahoma Land Rush of 1889. If you're fast enough, you can stake a claim. If you decide to wait until later, you'll be stuck with what's left over. Preparedness goes a long way toward success in the world of computers; if you can be one of the first people in line to offer a unique product or service, you can establish a foothold before anyone else has even thought to try.

> "M-commerce" (mobile commerce) is like the Oklahoma Land Rush of 1889. If you're fast enough, you can stake a claim. If you decide to wait until later, you'll be stuck with what's left over.

Still, no company should just jump blindly into the fray. Working quickly does not mean that you should be impulsive. Rather than running out immediately to stock up on WAP and WML manuals, start by conducting a thorough analysis of your unique situation. Indeed, the first order of business for any interested manager is to survey the field.

The Wireless Web Experience

In order make a prudent decision about your company's wireless readiness, you need a solid understanding of what differentiates the traditional Internet experience from the wireless version. As we mentioned briefly in Chapter 1, the mobile surfer is not conducting his search the way he would if he were searching the Internet from his home or office. He's typically in a different situation, working with a different set of goals and doing so with a far different tool at his disposal.

The Mobile Situation

It goes without saying that most wireless users are moving around—that's why we call it mobile computing. Even more than that, however, users are not usually focused on the computer itself. Generally, when a person at a desktop PC uses her computer, she's directing nearly all of her attention to the task at hand. She's stationary, normally indoors, and not unduly distracted by anything else going on.

Mobile computing is another story. Admittedly, when people use their cell phones or PDAs to access the Internet, they may actually be sitting quietly at home. But that's simply not the case the majority of the time. Cell phone and other handheld users are usually walking, driving, having a conversation, standing in line at the theater, shopping at the grocery store, or performing some other activity. They're doing all the little things that we do every day when we're away from home or the office. After all, if they were anywhere near a PC, they'd probably be using *that,* instead.

Because they're on the move, mobile users are also distracted. Or, to put it another way, they're multitasking pros. While they're attempting to surf the wireless Web, they're also continuing whatever behaviors or activities they had been engaged in prior to logging on. Take cell phones, for example. Although it might be wise to avoid driving and talking on the phone simultaneously, when's the last time you saw a car pull over so that the driver could answer his cell phone? Most people don't. They're either too impatient or too busy. It's important to understand, then, that the mobile surfer will often be trying to accomplish his online goals with one hand occupied—opening a door, carrying a briefcase, or carrying out some other activity—and most of his attention directed elsewhere.

The Mobile Mind-Set

Wireless Web users are also going online with an entirely different mind-set and goals than they would have if they were surfing from a wired terminal. Traditional Web surfing often involves either a certain degree of researching or aimless wandering. Especially in America, where Web access is not billed by the minute, time is not a huge factor while consumers are online. They may dislike waiting for pages to download, but they're also willing to look around different pages for additional product info, spend a half hour downloading a favorite song, or simply wander around hobby sites—wherever their fancy takes them. Wired Web surfing almost always involves one of the following activities: shopping for a product or service, doing research, or looking for recreation.

The wireless mind-set is very different. Because users are moving around, they're busy. And, because they're busy, they would not be going online unless they had a specific goal in mind. Mobile users know exactly what they want, and they want it as quickly as physically possible. They're in transition; they don't have time to waste waiting for pages to download or carefully searching for a product. They're in a hurry, and as a result they're extremely goal oriented. Wireless Web surfers want to log on, accomplish their mission, and log off so that they can continue with whatever else they were doing. The per-minute fees typical of wireless access add even more incentive for them to be brief. Waiting around or encountering delays is even more frustrating when the meter's ticking.

The Mobile Unit

The final circumstance that differentiates wired from wireless surfing is the computer's own physical form. Although we discussed several of these differences in Chapter 2, it helps to revisit some of them from the designer's point of view.

While desktop PCs have full-size screens, fast modems, vivid colors, and excellent graphics, today's handheld devices have a far more limited profile. First, they have small displays. Cell phone screens are particularly tiny—some of them can display only three lines of text, although newer phone screens are somewhat larger. The graphics are also limited; the resolution of handheld graphics leaves much to be desired. Although some PDAs can display color, most are black-and-white or grayscale. Even those that do have color usually have limited palettes. In addition, data entry is much more difficult. While desktop consumers can easily fill out forms and e-mail companies with product questions, mobile users are stuck using a numerical keypad or a stylus.

Finally, the data transfer rate on mobile units lags far behind that for their wired counterparts. This situation should improve in the near future, but for now slow access is a fact of life for wireless Web subscribers.

Effective M-Commerce Business

Since there's such a big gap between the wired and the wireless Internet experiences, it's important for enterprising business people to understand that what works for the wired surfer will not necessarily work for the guy on the subway. You should focus your efforts on services that take advantage of the wireless experience; in turn, you should either play down or avoid anything that doesn't work well with a mobile audience. There are two main ways to get in on the m-commerce boom: create a mobile start-up or adapt your existing business's storefront to wireless technology.

> Focus your efforts on services that take advantage of the wireless experience.

Start-Ups

Mobile start-ups are probably not the best course of action for most business people. They require a great deal of investment capital in order to get off the ground, profit margins are generally smaller, and they lack the strong existing customer base that brick-and-mortar companies have. For these reasons and more, start-ups have a high failure rate. They rarely ever make it out of the red—witness Amazon.com's notorious troubles. This doesn't require much elaboration. Unless you've been trapped under a heavy object for the past two years, you're almost certainly aware of the recent dot.com slump. Almost everyone knows the risks involved in creating an online business.

Still, this isn't to say that success is impossible. The cleverest (and luckiest) individuals who start mobile commerce companies early on have the golden opportunity to blaze a new trail. For that reason, we should at least briefly examine the kinds of businesses that will most likely be profitable on the wireless Web.

Entrepreneurs should look for ways to differentiate their company from the everyday virtual storefront. Since mobile customers are looking for different things than wired customers, the start-up should create a company that meets their special needs. This should be a specifically mobile site, not a regular Web site that also happens to be mobile. Such efforts should focus on offering niche services that cater exclusively to the primary concerns of wireless consumers.

Information

When wireless Web users take the time to log on in the middle of a busy day, they're generally not looking to accomplish a task that could wait until they get to their home or office. For one thing, the restricted nature of the handheld device means that surfing the wireless Web is a less satisfying experience; for another, remember that the wireless Web user is often occupied with other things. If Sue wants to buy a coat online, there's no pressing need for her to buy it from her PDA on the way to a meeting. She can either head to the mall later on or just shop online from her desktop PC once she gets home, with no per-minute charges and a superior visual experience.

No, wireless Web use will mostly be confined to tasks that must be accomplished immediately. Time will almost always be a factor. Therefore, shopping won't likely be one of the favorite wireless pastimes—at least, for the foreseeable future. Instead, the focus will be on information.

First, there's just general information. A student in class comes across an unfamiliar word in the textbook; with a wireless PDA, he can just look it up. A day-trader or stockbroker can keep an eye on market fluctuations twenty-four hours a day; a simple program can be created to beep the handheld whenever a price reaches a certain previously established threshold. In both of these situations, the wireless device comes in handy because the user does not have access to a desktop PC at the time the need arises. The device is useful because it's portable.

Wireless handhelds, however, have yet another ace up their sleeves. They can provide a much more valuable type of information—they can be location-specific. Remember that phones have the potential to pinpoint the user's exact location. This means that the owner can download information and be provided with results tailor-made to the very situation she's in at the moment the request was made. If a couple comes out of a matinee movie and decides to go for dinner, they can use a Web-enabled phone to look up some good local restaurants. Once they've settled on a restaurant, they may even be able to download the menu and make reservations. Hand-helds are also perfect vehicles for retrieving maps and driving directions from the Internet. Not only can the user get a map of the area, but, thanks to GPS technology, he can also download directions to his destination from *the very spot* where he's standing with the wireless device. Now *that's* personalization!

In all of these scenarios, it is either inconvenient or impossible for the consumer to use the wired Internet to fulfill her needs. People want immediate data in all kinds of situations where traditional methods are out of the question. This is where wireless technology can step in to fill the gap. Having a Web-enabled phone or PDA will soon be like having a dictionary, encyclopedia, atlas—your informational world in your pocket.

Entertainment

Although most people will use their wireless Web-enabled handheld to complete important tasks, there will also be a definite market for wireless entertainment. After all, consumers do spend a large part of their days either standing in line or waiting in traffic. Many PDAs already offer a variety of games to help their owners pass the time, but Internet access would really enhance the possibilities.

Web-enabled phones or PDAs can be used to download music directly from the Internet; although current handheld capacity severely restricts the amount of memory available for such pastimes, a few years will do much to alleviate the space squeeze. Soon people will be able to play several of their favorite songs on the go—downloaded to the cell phone, then wireless transmitted to small earphones. Who needs a landline to acquire MP3 tracks?

E-books should also prove popular. Many bookstores and entrepreneurs are already offering e-books at rock-bottom prices. A consumer is able to download a book for just a few dollars, read it, then delete the file to conserve memory. Having a book on your PDA will also minimize the amount of material you need to carry around. There's no longer any need to have that embarrassing summer page-turner tucked away in your briefcase at an important meeting; since you need your PDA with you anyhow, you might as well get some entertainment out of it!

Consumers will also be able to use their wireless link to play real-time games with people around the world; a PDA owner at a bus stop in Missouri will be able to engage in a poker game with competitors from Japan, Norway, and Italy. Users will simply pay to access the site that offers such links. Another company might allow consumers to subscribe to a daily e-mail: perhaps a joke of the day, a horoscope, or a favorite comic strip. Finally, the handheld user will be able to download games directly from the Web; he won't have to get them in advance from his PC's memory banks. When confronted with an unanticipated wait—perhaps at the airport—the wireless Web user can look around online for just the right game to pass the time. Many companies may create games designed specifically for handheld devices and store them on the Internet.

Finally, and more controversially, gambling will greatly benefit from wireless technology. OTB (Off-Track Betting) Web sites allow people to wager on races happening pretty much anywhere in the nation. For those racetrack aficionados who live too far from the track to make it on a regular basis, they can now place bets and check odds from either their wired PC or their wireless handheld. Sites such as US Off-Track are entirely legal (right now, anyhow) and enable visitors to gamble from a distance. Wireless technology allows people to stay up on the latest odds, then help them make better decisions. Many consumer groups disparage this latest use of wireless technology, but for now OTB stands firm.

Transactions

The third and final major use of wireless commerce will be based on transactions. Performing a transaction is an entirely different process from shopping; it involves known entities or commodities, so graphics and descriptions are of minimal importance.

For example, people will want to accomplish their banking over their cell phone or PDA; they'll be able to transfer funds, check their balance, order checks, and accomplish any number of important tasks without needing to be at home or at the office. Users will also be able to purchase just about any kind of ticket imaginable, so they'll be able to make it to the movie, concert, or show on the spur of the moment. Grocery shoppers will be able to pay for their purchases with their cell phones—right there at the checkout—already, some countries enable cell owners to buy from vending machines without cash, using only the phone keypad to make a choice.

Payments will become increasingly electronic in the wireless world; cash and check transactions are likely to become even more rare than they already are.

Wireless access allows the consumer to access the Internet in just about any conceivable situation. The entrepreneurial possibilities for wireless companies are similarly great; there are undoubtedly innovative services and niche markets for the wireless community that no one has even thought of yet.

> Wireless access allows the consumer to access the Internet in just about any conceivable situation.

Adapting Your Existing Business to the Wireless Web

The second option for businesses is a less glamorous but far safer route. Rather than start a new company from scratch, most businesses would be better off just altering their existing Web sites to accommodate wireless traffic. This is true for both purely virtual storefronts and for click-and-mortar businesses (those companies that have a real-world business as well as a Web site). It doesn't cost much in terms of time and money to adapt to wireless technology. This method also eliminates the chance of failure; since the business is already established in other areas, it doesn't need heavy wireless traffic in order to survive. Adding wireless capabilities to your existing Web site can only help your company.

If your company has not yet built a wired Web site, we strongly recommend that you create one—don't go directly from an off-line presence to a wireless-only profile. In the first place, there are *far* more consumers on the wired Web; wireless surfing is still a tiny percentage of overall traffic. Besides, the experience you get from working on the wired site will be invaluable in helping you decide how to create a wireless-friendly site.

Adapting your business could take the form of e-tailing, but that's pretty complex; selling items over the airwaves is a lot more complicated than it might seem at first. If you're determined to try it out, then you should make sure that you satisfy three conditions first:

1. You should already have a functional online purchasing site. If you haven't built one yet, then reconsider mobile sales for the time being. Making sales on the traditional Internet will provide you with the necessary experience.

2. Your service or product should be something that's easily sold in an extremely limited shopping environment. If you sell clothing, it's better to wait until cell phones and PDAs are better equipped for color, detailed graphics, photo, and/or video. Customers won't

want to buy items such as clothing when they can see it only pictured on a crude two-inch black-and-white screen.

3. Get some experienced tech support. If you're reading this book, then you're probably not an expert. Don't try to build a wireless Web purchasing site on your own. It would take you too much time to learn the details, and you're less likely to do a good job than someone who makes a living designing WML pages.

The wiser choice for most online businesses is to start with more modest goals. There are two kinds of services that you can easily provide online, without the hassle of selling products or providing financial processing. You can provide information, which is static, and you can offer more comprehensive customer support. We discuss basic wireless page design in Chapter 5 and customer support in Chapter 6.

Choosing a Wireless Standard

Even if you decide not to go mobile at all for the time being, it's important to at least know what options are out there. Sooner than you might think, wireless Web access will be mainstream, and companies will be scrambling to set up storefronts on the wireless Web just as they rushed to the Internet in the mid-1990s. If you stay up on mobile technology, then you minimize your chances of being caught flat-footed. When you eventually decide to make the leap, you'll be knowledgeable enough to develop a great strategy.

With the dizzying array of wireless constructs currently in use, choosing the language and protocol with which to build your wireless Web site is a lot more difficult than you'd think. Each year brings a new standard to the table, which is then adopted with varying degrees of success; making a decision is even more difficult when you consider that your choice might shut out a large percentage of the wireless market: Many of the protocols, although closely related, are not interoperable. Many WAP-enabled phones are not able to read HDML content. You'll thus want to keep your target market closely in mind when as you weigh your options.

HTML

HTML, or HyperText Markup Language, is the easiest language to use, simply because it's the standard language for the wired Internet. Just about every single Web page on the Internet today was built on HTML. All you need to do in this case is to keep some general guidelines in mind as you create the page; you could even settle for simply adapting your existing site.

Of course, there are significant drawbacks to using HTML as code for a wireless page. Wireless browsers use only material that is suitable for the reduced dimensions and computing power of their client handheld device. They are thus unable to recognize many of the tags, or special features supported by the HTML language. Bits of interactive programming, certain fonts, text effects, and table features simply do not show up on handheld devices. Unfortunately, since the source code includes them, this incompatibility leaves unsightly "holes" in the resulting page; the formatting is off, and the user may very well be treated to a confusing jumble of text and graphics.

C-HTML

C-HTML, or Compact HTML, was developed in 1998 by the World Wide Web Consortium (W3C). Around this time, HTML was becoming increasingly complex in order to cater to the correspondingly complex machines that were running the code. Yet this was also the time when handheld Web-enabled devices were first hitting the market. W3C realized that it would need to develop a special language for the smaller devices, something tailor-made for their reduced capacity and screen size. The resulting code was dubbed C-HTML. Although Europe and the United States have yet to embrace this particular language, it's still important in that it was the first popular mobile standard. To be more specific, it's popular in Japan, where millions of users subscribe to the ubiquitous imode service.

C-HTML is identical to HTML, except that it's simpler and more limited in scope. While HTML has come to include a variety of complicated tags and functions, C-HTML strips the language back down to the basics. The good news is that "basics" are pretty much all that you'll need with a handheld device. The inherent limitations of mobile units entail a certain degree of austerity in design—and C-HTML is more than up to this task. It can designate paragraph breaks, indentation, simple JPEG and GIF graphic formats, and more. On the other hand, it cannot specify font styles, frames, or the tables of which so many Web designers are fond. See Chapter 5 for more information on designing a C-HTML site.

C-HTML's main benefit is that it can be used for both wired and wireless Web sites. The programmer need only design one site for a particular company; C-HTML is amenable to virtually any kind of browser. Some companies balk at creating such a bare-bones Web site when most of their traffic is still wired; to resolve the problem, many businesses in Japan chose to create a separate C-HTML site for wireless traffic. That way, they did not have to tone down the extras on their standard page.

Imode

C-HTML's greatest advocate is imode. Even though the imode system exists only in Japan, it has become so popular that it warrants special discussion. DoCoMo has cornered more than 60 percent of the Japanese cell phone market, and more than 90 percent of the subscribers sign up for the imode Internet service. Compare these numbers with the 15 percent average international usage percentage from Chapter 1; such a large percentage is positively staggering. Why is wireless Internet access so successful in this particular country?

In the first place, imode provides dedicated access to

the Internet. Users do not need to log on and log off every time they need information. Getting Web access is as quick and immediate as clicking on the right button; having an imode phone is like having DSL in the palm of your hand. The modem is still a lot slower than its wired counterparts, but it's far superior to the existing "dial-up" European and American systems of wireless access.

Imode phones can also handle high-quality content. Unlike even the most advanced phones elsewhere, imode handsets can display color pictures, animated files, and simple sound programs. In other countries, Web-enabled handhelds are still restricted to monochrome text and only the simplest of graphics.

Another one of imode's advantages is the generous amount of content available to subscribers. Japanese companies have created myriad Web sites—at last count, more than 38,000—designed specifically for imode subscribers, all using the C-HTML language. The service has been so successful that even some foreign companies have posted their own imode sites: Disney, CNN, Dow Jones, and many more. But, despite the rich content available, imode is not restricted to official imode sites. It's flexible, capable of accessing regular Web sites as well. Regular Web sites may not appear as neatly as do imode screens, but they're still available to the DoCoMo subscriber. The imode portal simply filters out the data and graphics that it cannot support, then sends the stripped-down page to the client device.

Finally, we did mention before that it's cheaper for the Japanese to use cell phones than for them to surf online. Basic imode Web service runs to only about $3 per month—which is so cheap that it's almost imaginary. But that's not the only factor. Because imode provides dedicated access, there no sense in charging customers for the amount of time spent online; the phones are *always* online. Instead, they charge customers for the amount of data sent and received. The prices are more than reasonable. It costs only about two to five cents to send brief e-mail messages, and downloading pictures or graphics usually sets the user back less than a dollar.

In addition to the expected uses for research and for transaction-based services, many subscribers use the service as their main form of communication with colleagues and friends. Games and entertainment programs are popular, as well; imode users can sign up to have pictures or comics sent to them each day for a small fee.

Not surprisingly, all these factors make it the most influential wireless Internet service in the world. More important, in an unstable market, DoCoMo will likely remain powerful for years to come. It's a flexible company. No matter how successful its C-HTML sites have become, it's not content with the status quo. DoCoMo is working to ensure that WAP sites will be able to access imode material, and it's also investing heavily in the wireless version of Java. (We'll get to WAP and Java in just a bit.)

Regardless of how well C-HTML works for the imode service, however, it fails to address some problems. The compact format enables handheld devices to display the desired elements on-screen, but it does not provide for a universally clean layout. The language cannot describe itself, cannot instruct individual devices how to display the content.

In Japan, where content providers benefit from the near-ubiquity of imode access, this shortcoming does not matter that much. All DoCoMo handsets are fairly standard in design, which enables programmers to create a single site that will appear clean on all imode phones.

For Americans and Europeans, however, the situation is different. While a given document might appear perfectly centered on a Palm Pilot, it might look ragged on a cell phone, with bits of various lines strewn across the screen. If each country adopted a single handheld form, then C-HTML might work as well as it does in Japan. But, given the current multiplicity of PDAs, cell phones, and pagers, it's not likely to happen for many years, if ever. The rest of the world needs an alternative. Enter XML.

XML

XML was first developed by a Sun Microsystems engineer in 1996. At the outset, however, it wasn't viewed as integral to wireless content development. This isn't surprising; after all, just a few short years ago, wireless computing was still in an embryonic stage. Few people were thinking in mobile terms. Instead, the XML language was designed to improve wired programming.

Normal HTML tags designate the appearance of any given block of material. <Bold>Hello</Bold> would, on an HTML document, appear as: **Hello**. The <Bold> tag *describes* the content, but it cannot *define* the content. Any device that reads the language knows that the enclosed letters should be bolded, but it cannot explain or define what the data represent. At first glance, this doesn't appear to be a big deal. After all, who cares what the data represents? The reader knows, so why must the computer know?

One of the problems is that HTML is inflexible. Once the tags have been set, the client device is stuck trying to imitate the exact designated appearance of the original document. And, since the client can only blindly copy the content, it is unable to intelligently adapt the format. A document designed for a standard Internet Web page might very well wind up looking messy or stilted on a three-inch screen. Finally, if no HTML tag exists for a particular effect, the programmer is out of luck. XML adds a great degree of flexibility.

With the XML language, programmers are able to define their own tags, thus allowing for an infinite variety of content effects and forms. If no tag exists, they simply create a new one. More important, however, the tags refer to the content, rather than appearance. A sample XML tag might refer to <Salutation>Hello</Salutation>. Although the difference between form and content tags might seem negligible to many people, it makes all the difference to the programmer. Such tags enable the client device to *understand* the data that it displays. Instead of being forced to parrot the structure of an HTML program, the client can actually interpret the content and display it in the most appropriate manner for that particular device.

For example, in the case of the HTML tag for *hello*, all the client knows is that the enclosed figures should be bolded. It doesn't know anything else. Thus, if the line is transferred to a radically different setting, the client can't change the position of the salutation to best suit the host device. After all, it doesn't even know what the word represents! The XML sample tag, however, tells the client what the data *are*. The client can then use what it knows about the tag (which would have been defined elsewhere in the program) to display the information to the best effect. With XML, a document can be neatly displayed on anything from a laptop to a cell phone, with only minimal distortion. It's truly a powerful language, and some experts predict that XML is poised to dominate the field, especially since it's compatible with HTML.

VoiceXML

One version of XML is destined to become a major force in wireless programming: VoiceXML. VoiceXML was first conceived in 1995 by researchers from AT&T, Lucent Technologies, and Motorola. Although voice technology was only embryonic at the time, the researchers knew that, eventually, voice recognition programs would become accurate enough to be truly viable. The companies thus began working to develop a universal, voice-centric programming language. After all, if a Web site is to center around a voice interface, then the site also needs to be able to export the algorithms that will enable the program. Otherwise, if each company used its own, idiosyncratic language, client and server would be unable to understand one another.

If it becomes universal, as it likely will, VoiceXML will revolutionize wireless Internet use, just as HTML did the wired Internet. It will allow cell users to surf the Web, make transactions, find information, and accomplish any number of tasks—*all without pressing a single button*. VoiceXML is almost certain to take the world by storm.

XML is a universal language and is, therefore, capable of being used by virtually any device. Nevertheless, there are other, more narrowly applied languages in current use. In the earliest days of wireless, standards were often created for specific kinds of handhelds. As such, they have the ability to take advantage of the unique capabilities of a particular type of device. One such standard is Web-clipping.

> XML is a universal language and is, therefore, capable of being used by virtually any device.

Web-Clipping

Web-clipping is not a programming language. It's actually a proprietary technique employed to convert standard HTML Web pages to a format suitable for viewing on a handheld. Web-clipping was created by 3COM, the large parent company that manufactures the popular Palm computers; more specifically, it was developed for one handheld in particular, the Palm VII.

Although Web-clipping is not likely to ever become a mainstay of the wireless browser market, it still merits a brief look. After all, Palm VII computers were, for a time, the most popular Web-enabled PDAs on the U.S. market.

As a result, every business should at least know what the technique is.

Web-clipping originates with a special application built in to certain Palm devices. Not surprisingly, it's called the Web Clipping Application, or WCA. (The program used to be known as the Palm Query Application, so don't be surprised if you run across this name in older texts.) The WCA is actually a repository for specially-formatted, highly condensed Web pages. It modifies and holds stored, or "cached," Web information. This comes in handy when a user wants to view Web material either minutes or days after first accessing it; unlike PCs, which cache pages only during a particular session, the Palm's WCA stores the information permanently on the hard drive. If a user downloads a city map of New York while still in California, he can break the connection, knowing that he can immediately recall the specified pages when he needs them.

Basically, this is how it works: When a user requests certain information, the WCA first checks its memory files; if the correct pages have already been downloaded, then the WCA merely displays the appropriate content in a format designed for the Palm device's dimensions. If the WCA browser cannot find the URL in its own files, then it connects to a special proxy server. The proxy server requests the material from the Web, then strips it down—clips it—to a Palm-acceptable format. The proxy then forwards the altered material to the Palm device, which then both displays the page(s) and caches the URL for potential later use.

Another benefit of Web-clipping is that it can capture several pages at once; once the user has accessed a particular site on the Web, she can disconnect with the knowledge that she can survey the entire site later at her leisure—it's all stored on her Palm.

The main problem with Web-clipping is that it's complicated to make a request. Each request for information must be generated in the form of a special "palm query"—which the user must program himself, each time he wants to access a Web site. This can be a bit of a pain even for experienced programmers, and for novices it's even worse. Although the queries are relatively simple in format, they're still time-consuming. So, although Palm VIIs are around in sufficient numbers to make WCA a factor, it's not going to be taking over the world anytime soon. Most countries outside the United States haven't even heard of Web-clipping.

HDML

HDML, or Handheld Device Markup Language, was the first mobile solution to make a solid break from HTML. C-HTML and Web-clipping were designed to make standard web pages fit handheld devices; because they entail a certain amount of squeezing and reformatting, they are rather stop-gap solutions. HDML was the first attempt to create a language intended specifically for handheld use. Unwired Planet unveiled the language in 1996, and for a brief time it was the most popular mobile tongue.

Like C-HTML and WCA, HDML eschews the use of complicated programming features, such as frames, flashing fonts, complex graphics, and other extras not suited to the handheld profile. Yet HDML's most significant innovation was its use of a new programming infrastructure. Rather than building Web pages, programmers would design "cards" and "decks."

The change came about when Unwired Planet noticed that a standard Web page is complex enough to constitute a single file. When the browser downloads a batch of material, its "bite," so to speak, is large enough to grab only one page at a time. With handheld devices, however, the situation is entirely different. Handheld devices can only display a little bit of material at once; the screens are simply too small to display an entire Web page. Nevertheless, the microbrowsers working for a Web-enabled phone or PDA have approximately the same capacity as standard browsers; if they are asked to download only one handheld screen at a time, they end up working far short of their potential.

HDML takes advantage of this situation. Rather than downloading only one screen, it downloads a batch of several small screens at once; each screen is referred to as a "card," each batch is called a "deck." In this way, the browser is working to capacity while still keeping the format to handheld dimensions. While surfing the wireless Web, then, a user does not need to wait for every single screen to download. He can click through several cards before the browser needs to request a new deck.

Programmers refer to a single card as a "user interaction." In other words, a card presents information to the user and then requires the user to interact with the device in order to proceed. Because handheld displays are so small, cards are almost always limited to one in-teraction. Normal cards can take one of three different forms:

1. **Text-Only.** These cards merely display a certain amount of information. The only interaction that takes place occurs when the user clicks on the option to proceed or to move to the next card. Consider a wireless user who is checking movie reviews. After clicking on a particular title, the next card merely displays static information about the movie.

2. **Selection.** Selection cards allow the user to choose an option from a list of possibilities. At the same movie site, perhaps, the user might be presented with a list of all the films currently showing at a particular the-ater. The surfer would then dial or click on a certain choice, which would then bring her to the next ap-propriate card—in this case, one that displays show times for the selected movie.

3. **Input.** Data-entry cards are the final type. They ask the user to input a specific type of information, whether alphabetic or numeric. If that same surfer wanted to bring up a list of theaters in her area, for example, she could enter her zip code into the proper field on the card. Banks could request either account or credit card information, wireless dictionaries might require the user to enter the desired word.

    Because input cards require the greatest degree of interaction and concentration from the user, they are also to be used only when necessary.

HDML, then, revolutionized handheld programming languages. While other efforts sought merely to cover up or minimize the limitations of wireless devices, HDML built them into strengths. Nevertheless, it wasn't perfect. Before long, a unified protocol for wireless devices was created. The standards were developed by a group of companies looking for a true wireless protocol: They constituted the WAP forum. The forum created and espoused a new language, so HDML has been relegated to the sidelines.

WAP

Wireless Application Protocol (WAP) arose in 1997 from the tangle of competing wireless standards. Many companies had proposed languages and standards for global wireless communication, but they could not agree on a particular plan of action. Each had a pet project that could possibly work but found it difficult to get the others to adopt its proprietary plan. One thing became clear: Standards are impossible if there's no consensus.

Finally, several of the wireless giants agreed to work together on a new standard. In 1998, this WAP Forum debuted the first version of the new protocol: WAP 1.0. WAP is not a programming language; it's an all-encompassing platform standard for wireless communications. The WAP standard sought to impose rules, to bring order to chaos. WAP applies to many different areas of wireless technology; in fact, it's supposed to be a "seven-layer" standard, although it seems nobody can agree exactly about what those layers are. The rules and applications of each WAP layer are detailed and unbelievably technical; we could spend the rest of this book just talking about them. Not that we'd want to.

There's good news, however. No average business person needs to understand the differences between the Data Link Layer and the Session Layer. The only thing you need to know is that WAP imposed a broad, much-needed standard on nearly every aspect of wireless communication. Oh, and it gave birth to WML.

WML

WML, or Wireless Markup Language, is the flagship programming language for the WAP standard. In other words, WAP establishes a large number of rules for wireless, one of which is that devices communicate in WML.

WML is actually based on HDML, Unwired Planet's early success story. Programmers also borrowed from XML, in that WML allows programmers to define their own tags. This was considered particularly useful because handheld devices are so different in both form and capacity. PDAs and Web-enabled phones are both included in the general category of "handheld," but they have markedly different displays and memories—and that's not even taking into account the differences among manufacturers. XML allows devices more elbow room in displaying content so that each brand can make the most of its unique dimensions and capabilities.

WML is thus a hybrid: It borrows the HDML card/ deck method, but it's much more flexible, like XML. Outside Japan, almost all microbrowsers currently on the market adhere to WAP, whether it's the initial 1.0 standard or the latest version. If you're planning to market a wireless Web site in the United States or Europe, it definitely needs to be WAP-compatible. The best feature of WML is its flexibility. Any page written in WML looks good on whatever device downloads it, because WML allows the client device to format the page before displaying the results. HTML and HDML try to force square pegs into round holes and often wind up with incoherent results. WML lets the handheld decide what shape the peg should be. Sometimes, one size can actually be made to fit all!

For now, WML is king of the wireless hill. Companies are scrambling to ensure that they are WAP compliant, and the latest handheld devices, especially cell phones, which have so embraced the standard that they are often referred to as WAP-enabled, rather than Web-enabled.

But no victory is guaranteed. The different versions of WAP are incompatible with one another, which means that many so-called WAP-enabled phones are actually not interoperable. Its utility might also be short-lived: 3G phone systems and revamped PDAs might eventually be able to handle the full-strength Internet, without the need for a stripped-down standard. Finally, there are a few competitors looking to steal some of WAP's undeniable thunder. J2ME is the most likely contender.

J2ME

J2ME—also known as Java 2 Micro Edition or JavaLite—was recently launched by Sun Microsystems, the well-known Java developer. (The introduction, surprisingly, has helped the language come full circle: The Java language was originally conceived as a platform for portable devices.) Java is a solidly universal language; virtually any device can read it.

J2ME has more programming muscle than WML because it will be able to run scaled-down versions of popular Java applications—Calculator and Expense Pad, for example. It can also display far more sophisticated graphics, and in brilliant colors.

The problem, of course, is the sheer power necessary to run even a "lite" version of the language. Despite Java's universality, reading the language is only part of the process. Actually running the program is an entirely different matter. Early Internet-ready handhelds were simply too limited to process Java programs. That situation is changing, but slowly. J2ME-capable phones are still new to Europe and are just barely beginning to hit the U.S. market. One of the first offerings, Nextel's i85s phone, became available only in the middle of 2001, far behind the WAP products. J2ME obviously has a lot of catching up to do.

Nevertheless, many large cell phone manufacturers are banking on it. They're confident that the upcoming 3G phones will be equal to the task of handling such a powerful language. Nextel, Nokia, Sony, Motorola, and Japan's NTT DoCoMo are all to some degree supporting the J2ME system. Java is also trying to minimize the amount of space it takes up on the user's memory. The J2ME edition stores only essential programs locally on the wireless device; all other features are downloaded on an as-needed basis from a wireless Web site. Whether it will be able to overtake the popular WAP standard—or whether the point will be moot in a few years—is anyone's guess.

Which Choice Is the Right One?

Given the dizzying variety of mobile languages currently on the market, how can anyone decide which to choose? Although some platforms are more widespread than others, there's no clear winner—and, to make matters worse, almost all of them are incompatible. It seems that no matter what language a company eventually decides to run with, it's going to be excluding a large percentage of potential customers. WML may fit the bill for many consumers, but it leaves HDML and J2ME users out in the cold.

The best tactic, it seems, for a few companies, is to cover all the bases: Some businesses have simply created more than one Web site. Of course, most people have neither the time nor the resources to develop alternate Web pages; as small as the wireless market currently is, the return on investment would be hideous.

When all else fails, examine your customer pool. Of course, it may be hard to predict what—if any—type of wireless devices your clients own. In that case, ask them directly! Survey your regulars by either polling them on location in the store or by e-mailing them. Just make sure that you do it right: Lots of companies have trouble with surveys because they always generate an extremely low response rate. (Small samples are known to run the risk of yielding bad data.) To encourage responses, try offering an incentive or freebie to those who reply, perhaps a discount or an inexpensive, overstocked product. People are more likely to participate if there's a tangible reward. Here are some of the questions you might want to ask:

- Do you currently have wireless access to the Internet?

- If you do not have wireless access, do you intend to have it in the near future?

- If you have wireless access, what type of device do you use? How often do you use it?

- What tasks or activities do you participate in while wirelessly online? Business? Shopping? Communication? Information searches?

The key is to be *prepared*, not hasty.

Once you've got the results, look for trends. Are your customers mostly cell users? Go with WML. High-end, techie cell users? Try a J2ME-compliant page. Palm Piloteers? No worries—Web-clipping will take care of the work for you. If all else fails, C-HTML will be technically functional for just about any wireless browser. Just don't expect your customers to see the same, neatly arranged Web site that PC surfers do—the format might be a tad "off."

And if your customers aren't using wireless devices

at all? Relax, there's no rush. Just keep a sharp eye on their habits and the ever-changing market, and be prepared to expand to wireless whenever it becomes practical to do so. Remember, the key is to be *prepared*, not hasty.

Chapter 5

Implementing Your M-Commerce Plan

You basically have two options when deciding who should write the material for your wireless Web site. Some companies choose to hire an outside expert, a programmer who specializes in handheld content. Others assign the task to an IT employee already on staff. There are advantages and disadvantages to either choice, and we will explore both options.

Outsource or In-House?

As you decide whether to use in-house personnel or to go outside to create your wireless Web site, these are a few of the points you should consider:

Outsource

If you run a particularly small business, then you'll probably want to outsource the mobile Web site. It's far easier to rely on an experienced individual who has already mastered the techniques particular to wireless content.

You shouldn't hire the first person that comes along, however. Shop around for the right person, and don't be afraid to be picky. A good wireless content programmer should provide a list of sites he has produced or built. Ask for it, and personally examine each site. The sites should be highly polished and functional; you should feel comfortable navigating; and you should be easily able to find specific information. This isn't the time to be giving someone new a try; don't risk your reputation on someone who is untested, even if he's cheaper than the competition.

> If you run a particularly small business, then you'll probably want to outsource the mobile Web site.

A few things to be aware of: Outsourcing can be more expensive, since the experts generally charge by the hour—and the best charge more than the rest. You should be prepared to pay more than you would a salaried employee. In addition, outside experts are not as familiar with your company. As a result, you'll want to stay involved in deciding what material should and should not be included on the wireless site. Don't just hand the project over and forget about it. The programmer should have a final say in technical matters, but you should feel comfortable with the overall design and intent. After all, it's *your* company, and you know your customers better than anyone else.

In-House

Your other option is to allow one or two current IT employees to develop the site. If you have a full technical staff, then it's not too difficult to assign experienced individuals the task of developing content for a mobile Web site. Allow them plenty of time to become familiar with the wireless languages—probably C-HTML, WML, and J2ME—and work closely on the general site design with them. If you provide them with a clear plan and goal, then they should be able to execute with a minimum of fuss. Still, restrict your involvement to broad, design-oriented issues. Avoid interfering in the technical details; micromanaging will only annoy your staff and slow the project.

The good news is that using your own employees is cheaper than outsourcing, and they're also familiar with your company from the inside. You won't need to waste a lot of time acquainting a stranger with the intricate workings of your business; your employees already know—and they presumably have accumulated valuable experience developing and maintaining your wired Web site.

The main risk with internal development is lack of experience. Although allowing your own people to design the site is considerably cheaper, they also don't have the solid wireless experience that the freelancers do. Unless they're incredibly motivated, they probably will need to start learning wireless programming from scratch. HTML is similar to WML, but there's still a learning curve to consider.

Whichever option you choose, you'll still need to have a good idea of what content to include in your site, as well as how that material should be presented.

General Do's and Don'ts

Most Internet experts advise companies to stick with the simplest possible arrangement for their wired Web sites. Although the myriad available options, applications, programs, and other gewgaws can be tantalizing, the company should abstain from using too many, or else it risks overloading the page. Consumers desire clarity and speed above all else, we are told. And it's true. And, for the wireless Web, such guidelines are even *more* valid.

The following advice is general, in that it applies to virtually any mobile Web site, no matter what language the page uses.

Keep It Short

If brevity is a virtue on the wired Internet, it's even more vital for the wireless world. Text should be minimal. Part of the reason is the same as for home PCs: The screen breaks up the material, making it difficult to see the piece as an organized whole. The longer the passage, the more it's adversely affected by display size. Therefore, you should keep your sentences as short and direct as possible. Since cell phones and PDAs have even smaller screen than do desktops, this is obviously a key issue.

> If brevity is a virtue on the wired Internet, it's even more vital for the wireless world.

But wordiness is also a handheld drawback for a very different reason: attention span. When a PC user is surfing the Web, he probably has most of his attention focused on the monitor. He reads everything at once, from start to finish. With handhelds, it's an entirely different situation. People scanning wireless Web material will likely be reading in brief bursts. They might glance at the screen for a few seconds, become distracted for a few moments, then glance back at the text, then away, then back, and so on. In other words, wireless devices often do not have the full attention of the user.

Lengthy sentences and paragraphs are then a doubly bad idea. They take a long time to digest; they're difficult to grasp in a few bite-sized pieces. Wireless users are not looking for a dissertation on the various sociological effects of European imperialism on the African continent. They just want to know whether the stocks are up, or whether the movie got a good review. Don't say more than you absolutely must.

Narrow It Down

In addition to keeping your text short, you'll also want to watch your breadth. When creating a wireless card or page, keep the columns from getting too wide. While traditional PCs have either square or wide rectangular displays, most handhelds have longer, skinnier screens; some permit only thirty-two characters to the row. Such a format is not ideal for broad paragraphs; the lines wind up getting cut off from the main display. Text that spills off the screen looks messy, and it makes it difficult for the user to grasp the message. Some programmers might think it a necessary trade-off in quality, however. They feel that it's even more important to keep the whole body of text "above the fold" in the screen, so it's worth the risk.

Remember that wireless users are often distracted; if they have to scroll over to finish every single line, they'll lose continuity. And that's the *best*-case scenario. At worst, they'll become frustrated enough to try a different site or log off entirely. Besides, some cell phones don't even have a horizontal scrolling option; your reader would then be incapable of moving the view to the right. Virtually every Internet handheld, however, is able to scroll down. In addition, scrolling down doesn't disturb continuity nearly as much as scrolling across does; most lines are intact, thus conveying its meaning on one screen. Too-wide paragraphs cut virtually every line short. Therefore, it's a good idea to keep your columns narrow.

Free the Browser

Programming languages allow designers to specify what their creation's exact appearance will be. There are tags for font, spacing, and just about every other format quality a page could possibly have. Because they want to ensure a unified, clean storefront, most Internet programmers are careful to dictate the exact layout of each page. This ensures a quality result. PCs, no matter what make or model, all have a similar viewing environment, so the page is almost guaranteed to look the same regardless of which display downloads it.

Wireless Web sites, however, are a different story. Since the client units are so dissimilar, it's impossible to know in advance what appearance might be best suited for each particular device. Actually, no one appearance *at all* will be ideal in all situations. For example, most phones carry a limited number of font styles, so if the site specifies Book Antiqua, it might only cause trouble for a device that can't display the desired typeface.

Microbrowsers are actually able to stand on their own feet in such situations. Many users or programmers are able to set default settings for their own particular client device, ensuring that downloaded material will be displayed to the greatest advantage for that particular environment. It makes for an easy solution to the format problem: Let the receivers worry about how to display the page. They'll do a far better job of hand-tailoring the site than your Webmaster can, especially if he's trying to make the site work for two dozen different display configurations all at once. This is exactly why the WML language is becoming so popular—because it's flexible. Don't make the mistake of trying to orchestrate every little detail. It may work for desktop PC displays, but it'll only cause problems for handhelds.

Avoid Graphics

One of the standard rules of the Internet is to avoid using too many graphics. Well, it's true for the wireless Web as well—only it's more extreme. Don't use graphics unless there's a pressing need. In other words, you probably don't need the graphics that you'd love to include; actually, very few companies truly need pictures or icons on their wireless Web pages. People just *like* to have them. Of course, they can convey important information. But they're also fun to work with, they make sites more attractive, and they provide a fuller Internet experience. On a wired desktop, graphics are often a good idea, as long as the designer doesn't overload the page with colorful clutter. Too many pictures make the page look messy, and they cost even more in download time. Still, most Web sites could benefit from a simple, attractive graphic or two. With the wireless Web, however, the story's a lot different.

Mobile devices are still limited in lots of ways, many

of which make it difficult to display good pictures. For one thing, they have smaller, more rudimentary displays, which make high-quality graphics all but impossible. Pixel counts on handheld computers still lag far behind those for their desktop counterparts. In addition, nearly all PDAs and cell phones are black-and-white or grayscale, so they can't display colors of any kind. No matter how great the graphic is on a full-sized screen, it just doesn't turn out very well on the receiving end of a wireless hand-held device.

Next, the average mobile modem connection is far slower than the average wired device. If download time is important on the wired Web, it's at an even greater pre-mium for wireless consumers. What takes ten seconds to load on a 56K modem will usually take at least four times as long on a handheld device. And the user isn't waiting patiently. Mobile users are even worse than the average wired surfer. They don't want to sit around for thirty seconds, much less two or three minutes, waiting for a page to load just because it has a fancy picture on it. They'll only become frustrated and either go elsewhere or dis-connect.

> If download time is important on the wired Web, it's at an even greater premium for wireless consumers.

Finally, the consumers just don't care. While atmos-phere and general appearance might make somewhat of an impression on the traditional Internet, they don't have any relevant meaning for the wireless user who is surfing with a Post-it-size black-and-white screen while walking down a busy street, or even driving. This person is not looking for a visually exciting experience—she just wants to get in, get her information, and get out as quickly as possible. Adding graphics won't likely impress anybody, but it can always cause plenty of irritation.

There are only two current acceptable uses for graphics on the wireless Web: if you simply can't express your meaning without one or if the picture will take up less space than you would take up in words to get your point across. In either case, keep it as simple as possible. Black-and-white icons are preferred, though you can use a few bold colors if you really have a burning desire to do so. No matter what, make sure that the image won't take too long to load. However important your picture is, it can't make your case if no one sticks around long enough to see it.

Turning HTML into C-HTML

The easiest way to make your company mobile-friendly is to produce a C-HTML site, either by stripping your existing site down to the basics or by creating a separate C-HTML site especially for wireless Web surfers. This route is simple mainly because your tech staff doesn't need to learn a new language; it just needs to find out which HTML features do and do not function in a compact environment, then act accordingly. As a manager, you should also have a good idea of what C-HTML can accomplish.

Valid C-HTML Tags and Functions

The following list contains a series of HTML tags that is fully supported by C-HTML and thus can be used on your wireless Web site:

- **Paragraphs and line breaks.** You can separate groups of text and place spaces where appropriate.

- **Hyperlinks.** You can include hyperlinks, whether embedded in ordinary text or listed separately. Users will be able to click through the HTML links to other Web sites.

- **Input forms.** C-HTML supports HTML code that provides forms. Forms are lists of finite choices or empty fields that enables users to input data or other text into the site. C-HTML can process such input as usual.

- **Images.** C-HTML also allows for simple images in the GIF or JPEG formats. Nevertheless, you'll want to keep such images to a minimum. Even though C-HTML can technically handle these items, they still take a long time to load, and the wireless environment is not yet friendly to graphics.

Invalid C-HTML Tags and Functions

There are several more complex HTML functions, however, that simply cannot be supported by the compact versions. If any of the following tags currently exist in your Web site, you'll need to either remove them or develop an alternate site that does not include them. You can consult your IT staff on the specifics.

- **Tables.** Tables are an HTML structure used to support and organize data. If you're unsure whether they're used on your site, ask your tech staff; you won't be able to keep them for the C-HTML version.

- **Frames.** Frames are used to allow the user to view several windows of information simultaneously. Given the limited capacity and display of handheld devices, frames are simply impractical on the mobile Web. This also explains why C-HTML can't support them.

- **Programs.** Traditional applets and scripting languages (such as Java) are too complex for C-HTML. If you need these more powerful functions, you'll need to go the extra mile and program your site with either WML (which supports a special WMLScript) or J2ME (which supports a compact JavaScript). If you want to stick to an HTML-based language, you'll have to get rid of the programs on your site.

- **Font.** C-HTML does not permit font tags, whether they refer to size or typeface. Instead, in such cases the client device chooses an appropriate font style. Text effects aren't supported either—you can't have, say, bold or italic text. Your written content will necessarily be uniform in appearance.

- **Content tags.** Finally, C-HTML cannot employ tags that describe content or meaning. Unlike XML or WML, the tags can refer only to appearance and layout; they cannot describe the meaning of the data itself. A tag such as <Salutation>Hello</Salutation> is impossible with C-HTML. If your programmer needs such tags, you'll need to use a more flexible language.

No matter how limited C-HTML is, it's still a useful language. It enables companies to adapt a single site to both wired and wireless consumers, and it allows programmers to avoid learning new, more complex languages. If your site is a simple one—that is, if it is fairly static or if it doesn't require much user interaction—then C-HTML is a good wireless solution for your company. It requires the least amount of valuable time and human resources.

On the other hand, if your company has a more complex Web page, then you'll want to consider both of the most popular, more powerful options: WML and J2ME sites.

Designing a WML Page

If your site is complex, or if your customers will mostly be mainstream cell phone users, then you'll probably want to create a WAP page, using the WML language. After all, WAP was created specifically with phones in mind; PDAs can support WML, but it's not optimal for those particular devices. Unlike C-HTML's stop-gap solution, WML was tailor-made from the start for mobile computers.

The User Interface

First things first: C-HTML does not have a specific audience; it can be used for cell phones, PDAs, pagers, or laptops. With WML, however, you do have a group of target users: people with WAP-enabled phones. When creating a WML page, then, you'll want to consider the probable user interface. Most users will have WAP-enabled cell phones, which means that the data entry options are limited to the following:

- **Keypad.** All cell phones have numeric keypads; all WAP-enabled phones will have a certain number of letters above each key. The keypad thus allows users to enter numbers and—with more difficulty—text.

- **Special-function keys.** These keys are generally located just above or below the keypad. They can include SEND, CLEAR, POWER, SHIFT, and other generic operations; they can vary in minor ways from phone to phone.

- **Soft buttons or keys.** Soft keys are located just below the display. There are usually two of them, one on each side of the screen. They are unlabeled by the phone manufacturer; instead, the soft keys are assigned meaning by the WML document. They generally represent blanket commands, such as ACCEPT, BACK, or OPTIONS. The role they play for each card appears at the bottom of the screen, just above the appropriate button. Thus, on one card a soft key might be labeled ACCEPT and on the next card be transformed to OPTIONS.

- **Directional arrows/scrolling button.** All Internet phones allow the users to move around on screens with more than one option. "Navigation" tools can take a few different forms. Some phones use simple directional arrows, as on a standard PC keyboard. Others have rocker pads, an oval button that can be tilted to represent a direction. Finally, a few companies, such as Nokia, use rollers either on the front or side of the phone to allow for easy scrolling and selection.

WAP 1.1 Capabilities

WAP 1.1, the most recent version of the protocol, is capable of supporting several different operations. Keep this in mind as you develop the site; you may be surprised at what the language can and cannot do.

- **Text.** This one is obvious and requires no further explanation.

- **Graphics.** WML is able to support simple graphics; most of the time they need to be either black-and-white or greyscale, and very simple.

- **Animation.** Animation is possible, but only on the most basic level—a few frames per image at most. This will improve as time passes.

- **Links.** Just as on a regular wired Internet site, a user will be able to view and click on pretty much any link provided.

- **Input.** Users are allowed to enter information, either through list selection or by text entry.

- **WMLScript.** WML, like standard HTML, cannot think for itself. It cannot calculate data or process information. On the simplest Web sites, such as those that merely present information, this is not a problem. But, for more sophisticated pages, such as those that need to validate customer information, it's a major stumbling block. Enter WMLScript.

   WMLScript is a scripting language, similar to JavaScript. WMLScript can create programs; they are downloaded by the client device and executed in that local environment. Because wireless devices have a very limited processing capacity, WMLScript is an especially streamlined language, so that it can be downloaded with relatively little difficulty. Also, because it can be run on the client device, it's fast—there's no waiting for results from the server. The client performs its own calculations instead of requesting them from cyberspace.

   WMLScript is a key development because it gives the WML system needed programming muscle. C-HTML, without a special scripting language, cannot compete with this newer system. It is relegated entirely to more rudimentary Web sites.

J2ME

It's a lot more difficult to explain how to integrate Java code and programs into your Web site. While the other systems are meant to function in a specific page or environment, Java's main advantage lies in its universality: It is normally used as part of another document, perhaps HTML or WML, to either interface between incompatible page elements or to import powerful programs and applications.

The Java Virtual Machine

A large part of Java's independence lies in its portability, or ability for a single application to be run in virtually any kind of programming environment, from PCs to Macs to a variety of handheld devices. All any platform needs to run Java is a Java Virtual Machine.

A virtual machine, or VM, is special software that transforms and executes Java applications. It acts as a type of mediator; the VM is capable of interfacing with all major platforms. All you need to do is install it, which is incredibly easy for pretty much any programmer. The virtual machine provides for Java's independence, or portability.

J2ME Applets and Smart Cards

In a standard Java environment, the Java programs are stored in the desktop's memory. This isn't possible on more limited devices; they don't have sufficient capacity. J2ME compensates for this obstacle by storing only the most essential features locally on the device. All other programs and applets can be obtained in two ways—they can either be wireless downloaded, or they can be obtained from a Java smart card.

Java smart cards can carry a number of selected Java applets on a single card; the card can then be added to the handheld through either a smart card slot (these are usually found in cell phones) or with the help of a smart card reader inserted into the standard PC card slot. Without any need for the programmer to add anything, a smart card can enable a handheld device to perform such complex functions as wireless payment and games. J2ME allows Java to find a place on even the most limited devices.

Structuring Your Wireless Web Site

Whether you've outsourced the content development to a tech company or assigned it to your own IT staff, no matter what programming language you choose, you'll want to be involved in the general design of the site. As a manager, you know best which applications or services are important and which should be left off the page. Remember the limitations of the mobile medium: Your wireless Web site should be far simpler and more direct than your wired one; your customers won't be patient enough to wade through card after card of unnecessary information.

No matter what programming language you choose, you'll want to be involved in the general design of the site.

Flash Screens

If you really want a nice title page with your logo and slogan, then you should think about adding a brief flash screen to the site. A flash screen is a card or page that is displayed to the user for about one to five seconds, after which a new card is shown automatically. Since the wireless browser downloads an entire deck in one try, there shouldn't be any unforeseen delay between the flash screen and the card immediately following it. You can therefore brand your company name with the customers, and they won't need to click on anything. All they have to do is wait an extra couple of seconds. Nevertheless, it's a tricky gamble. Be sure that the flash screen really is a "flash." If your make your customers wait an excessive amount of time to get to the main page, they'll be irritated. No flash page should last longer than five seconds.

Home Page

Your main or home page should be more a table of contents than anything else. It should list clearly and cleanly the main options of your Web site so that the user can easily scroll down the list and click on her choice. Do not include any extraneous information whatsoever—no unnecessary graphics, fun facts, polls, lengthy text, or fancy design styling. Your customer is busy and probably distracted, so every function should be immediately apparent. Wherever possible, keep options to a self-contained list. Finally, try to keep each option to a single line, to draw the clearest line possible between one function and another.

Structure

The rest of the site should be formatted in a similar fashion, with the overriding design goal of moving from the general to the specific. Each card should have only one purpose, whether it's to have the user make a choice or to display information. Text should be limited to cases in which the viewer has specifically requested it.

For example, if your site offers movie reviews, keep each review on a separate card. Nobody wants to sift and scroll through reviews of every current show in order to find the only one she's interested in. Instead, start off with a general choice: New releases or older titles? On the next card, merely let the user select a letter of the alphabet. Once she's chosen that, you can provide a list of pertinent movies that begin with that letter. Finally, after the user clicks on a specific title, you can display the review. In this manner, users are presented only with information that they have explicitly requested. Never barrage your customers with unwanted data. It's both confusing and highly irritating.

Finally, always allow your users an "out." Whenever possible, have one of your soft key designations be BACK.

If a customer becomes lost or disoriented within the site, there should be a painless way for him to retrace his steps. If there's no turning back, he's likely to exit the site and try somewhere else. Also, post a customer support number or e-mail hyperlink wherever possible. It doesn't take up much space, and it provides immediate customer support.

Testing the Site

The Internet has a variety of Web sites devoted exclusively to wireless program testing. They imitate the function and capacity of a specific handheld device—usually cell phones—so that programmers can test their efforts in as realistic an environment as possible. There are too many sites for you to visit them all, but you should go to the ones that simulate handheld models that your customers are most likely to use.

Indeed, before you launch your site, it's imperative that you test it first. Then test it again, then again—until it works cleanly on almost any mainstream device. The following sections list some common development sites that support emulators for various mobile environments.

WAP Emulators

WAP emulators are browsers that, not surprisingly, simulate WAP phones. If your company is designing a site in

WML, then you should visit one or more of these simulators:

M3Gate. *www.numeric.ru*

Yospace. *www.yospace.com*

WinWAP. *www.winwap.org*

Up.SDK. *www.phone.com*

WAPEmulator. *www.wapmore.com*

J2ME Emulators

J2ME emulators work the same as the WAP versions, except that they support the Java environment:

Yospace. *www.yospace.com* (Yospace has both WAP and J2ME emulators.)

Motorola. *www.motorola.com*

Java. *developer.java.sun.com*

C-HTML Emulators

These sites emulate phones that work with C-HTML:

Microsoft Mobile Explorer. *www.microsoft.com/mobile/ phones* (This is pretty much your best bet. Most

C-HTML emulators are devoted to imode phones and are therefore in Japanese.)

PDA Emulators

Try these sites to test your wireless Web site for these PDAs:

PalmOS. *www.palmos.com*

Pocket PC. *www.pocketpc.com*

Security

As we mentioned in Chapter 3, security for mobile devices is an extremely serious issue. Wireless communications are notoriously public; there's no easy way to physically safeguard the signal, which can be either damaged or intercepted by outside parties. Security becomes particularly important in a public wireless environment. First off, there's e-mail communication between users on separate networks; it's important for companies to prevent transmission eavesdropping and hacking whenever possible. In addition, m-commerce is prey to fraud; when consumers are able to pay with a phone account, dishonest individuals will try to cheat the system.

Indeed, no matter how convenient they become, mobile computers will not be a significant means of communication or transaction until reliable safeguards have been developed—and firmly established.

Wireless Viruses

Although mobile computer viruses have yet to attack on a wide scale, they do exist. In June 2000, Spain experienced the world's first cell phone virus, Timofonica. The virus targeted Spain's largest wireless network, and it infected a large number of accounts before it was stopped. PDA worms and viruses have surfaced in recent years as well, reminding the market that wireless communications are not immune to the problem. A few companies have developed prevention systems, but the resulting programs are far from comprehensive.

Still, do the best that you can to protect any company mobile devices; some of the more dangerous viruses can destroy an entire network. You need to be aware of the danger and to try to avoid such an occurrence, but 100 percent prevention is impossible, especially right now. Expect further wireless antiviral programs in the near future; they are sorely needed in a nearly unprotected market.

Encryption

While those who create viruses are looking to damage and destroy information, other hackers just want to steal it. Wireless eavesdropping actually poses a far more serious threat than do the viruses because it compromises the business's and customers' personal records. Viruses seek and destroy without comprehension. Hacking enables breach of privacy and fraud. There's good news, however.

When it comes to hacking, we have far more advanced methods of prevention.

At first glance, wireless is particularly vulnerable. After all, analog signals are notoriously public; anyone with a shred of know-how can intercept and interpret these transmissions. But the introduction of digital telecommunications has enabled companies to add a serious layer of security; because the sound is transmitted in the form of numerical data, it can also be more easily protected.

The main way to prevent eavesdropping is to encrypt the transmission. Conceptually speaking, encryption is nothing new; people have been coding and cracking messages since time immemorial. But modern technology has enabled companies to install particularly complex encryption devices, which makes it more difficult than ever to intercept sensitive data. Although the technique is impractical with analog devices, it works exceedingly well with the latest digital technologies. Currently, there are two main types of encryption: symmetrical and asymmetrical.

Symmetrical Encryption

Symmetrical encryption means that the same key is used to both encode and decode a signal. Traditional codes have relied on this method for thousands of years; the signal is encoded with one particular key (or system), then decoded by a recipient who possesses the same key. The technique is reliable as long as the key is sufficiently complex.

Happily, modern technology is at the point where keys can be so sophisticated that they present trillions of possible combinations. As of 2001, not even the most powerful computers in the world can crack these—even if they had centuries to try. Symmetrical encryption is thus one of the safest forms of communication; it's possible to protect wireless signals.

Symmetrical encryption, however, isn't always the answer. Probably the most obvious, unavoidable problem is that both parties need to have the same key. And, in order to have the same key, one party must somehow convey it to the other. Herein lies the rub: In order to keep all future communications secure, one must keep the key secret. But how do you keep a signal secret when you haven't yet gotten that key to the other party? You have to somehow exchange the information in a secure manner, yet accomplish the task before the intended precaution is in place. Some companies solve the problem by delivering the key in person. But that's not always practical, nor is it foolproof. So, in recent years, programmers have developed a second major encryption method.

Asymmetrical Encryption

Asymmetrical encryption involves the use of two separate keys. In telecommunications, the most common system is Public Key Encryption, or PKE. PKE establishes both a public and a private key for each sender. The public key, true to its name, is available to anyone with whom that particular business or individual communicates. The other key is private, though it is tangentially related to the public version. Messages can be encrypted by virtually anyone with the public key but decoded only by the owner of the private key. But that's rather confusing. Perhaps an example will help.

Imagine that Sean decides to wirelessly e-mail Jason. Sean's message is automatically encoded with Jason's public key. The public key, true, is general knowledge, but, once encrypted, a message *cannot be decrypted without the private key*. It's like having a large store of open safeboxes available to all potential senders. Anyone can take an e-mail and place it in the box, thereby locking it. The lock is engaged easily, merely by closing the lid—this is like using the public key. Now, however, the contents of the box are secured. You can't open it without the right key—the private key. Sean's e-mail zips safely through the ether; nobody can crack the incredibly complex code without the right private key. Once it arrives at Jason's electronic doorstep, Jason opens and reads the message with his private key.

PKE eliminates that most common of symmetrical code problems: the insecure first communication. No matter whether it's the first, second, hundredth, or thousandth time the two parties have exchanged messages, PKE ensures that the information is always safely encrypted.

Since all of these exchanges take place in cyberspace, however, there still can be an element of uncertainty. You need to be sure that you won't be deceived by a false public key. Hackers are very good at what they do; without a safeguard, it would be possible for them to disguise their own public keys as those of a legitimate institution. An unwary business person might then encode and send a message to the wrong party; believing it to be addressed to one company, she instead encrypts it using the hacker's key. The message is then intercepted and read by the actual recipient—the hacker.

The Public Key Infrastructure, or PKI, was designed to prevent such fraudulent actions. The PKI establishes and verifies the public keys of various legitimate companies. Once it verifies the identity of the key owner, a telecommunications authority, called the Certification Authority, or CA, issues a certificate of authenticity. People can then send messages to the recipient, confident that the same recipient truly *does* hold the corresponding private key.

Encryption ensures that the transmission itself is secure. The PKI goes a part of the way toward establishing identity but stops short. It helps only in special cases, such as business e-mail. People also need to feel that their personal data are safe on their personal mobile devices.

If the PDA is lost or stolen, how can the owner make sure that his sensitive company data and personal address book are safe from prying eyes? In addition, cell phones and PDAs are increasingly becoming a form of payment, just like credit cards. How can companies ensure that unauthorized individuals can't start charging purchases to a stolen phone's account?

User Authentication

In the past, user authentication often required passwords, but passwords are becoming passé in mobile computing. Entering long strings of characters or letters into a cell phone is time-consuming; it also requires the user to pay close attention to the task at hand. It's a lot to ask of a harried person. Voice commands are going to be big, but don't expect voice-driven passwords any time soon, for obvious reasons. Nobody wants to speak his password into a phone while sitting on a crowded airplane.

Besides, in order to enter a password, one first has to remember it. People running to catch a bus don't usually have the necessary focus to recall an exact word or combination of numbers. And, if they've forgotten the password, the failure leaves them frustratingly unable to buy a ticket, or perhaps even to use their own computer! If they seek to avoid such situations by using the same easy password every time, they are vulnerable to hackers, who are experienced at guessing birthdays, pets, and favorite sports teams.

User authentication, then, is likely to settle on a technology that is both convenient and secure: biometrics. Biometrics involve the use of physical characteristics that are unique to each user, qualities that cannot be easily faked or imitated. The most commonly tested traits will likely be fingerprint, voice, and retinal identification.

- **Fingerprint scans.** Fingerprint ID will soon be a very popular security check. In the near future, many handheld devices will come equipped with a fingerprinting mechanism. Users will scan a fingerprint into their phone, PDA, or laptop when they first purchase the item, and this print will then be used to establish ID every time the user logs in or makes a purchase. It's incredibly effective, and the technology is already being used successfully on some desktop PCs.

- **Voice patterns.** Although voice-generated passwords will never be put to use, voice *itself* is a fantastic security device. Every single person's voice is unique in tone and pitch; it's nearly impossible to mimic someone's voice to the extent that a computer is fooled. Most voice ID scenarios involve a period in which the user trains the computer to recognize her voice by speaking a variety of words and phrases into the receiver. Once the computer has become comfortable with her speech qualities and patterns, it will be able to accurately identify her nearly all of the time.

  Though this particular test is still in developmental stages, programmers are working to improve voice ID accuracy to nearly 100 percent; however, until the technology is almost perfect, it can't be used as a form of identification.

- **Retinal scans.** The patterns of blood vessels in people's eyes are as unique to them as their fingerprints. Retinal scans are already used in certain high-security buildings, because they're nearly impossible for even the most talented hackers to fake. Retinal scans are likely to be introduced as security devices for handheld computers within the next few years.

Good wireless security must be established before mobile commerce can reach its full potential. The apparent vulnerability of wireless communication is a major obstacle for many companies; they simply do not yet feel comfortable making the transition to the wireless world.

All of this is understandable. After all, many of their

fears are grounded in fact; there still are definite weaknesses in wireless security. Nevertheless, mobile technology is becoming increasingly safe. Current encryption methods and imminent user authentication techniques are strong, reliable safeguards. They're not perfect, but neither are wired security measures; hackers still exist, despite our greatest efforts to thwart their intentions.

The fact is that the necessary technology is here, if businesses choose to take advantage of it. The only thing holding us back is our comfort level; as wireless devices become more common, people will feel more and more secure using them. Novelty can be a bit frightening. Once we see the wireless handheld as a familiar, established face, it will find acceptance in the market at large.

Chapter 6

Wireless Marketing

Wired marketing and wireless marketing are strikingly different practices. Although both involve the use of computers to advertise products or services, they have surprisingly little else in common. While Internet marketing transformed the face of twentieth-century commerce, mobile advertising promises to be just as revolutionary. Astute businesspeople should be alert and prepared: The wireless world presents an entirely new, exhilarating field of opportunities—but not without some serious risks.

Advantages of Wireless Marketing

Wireless advertising gives companies incredible sales power. Unlike traditional print, TV, or even Internet advertising, companies can now reach customers twenty-four hours a day—immediately, no matter where they are. They also know more about their client pool than ever before; they can discover their clients' habits, personalities, and lifestyles. It's a potent scenario, one that marketers have dreamed about for ages. Let's examine the situation more thoroughly.

> Wireless advertising gives companies incredible sales power.

Knowledge

As mentioned briefly in Chapter 2, handheld computers are usually personal communication and time management devices. Since each is owned by a single person, the ways the PDA or cell phone is used, the data downloaded and the phone numbers called can reasonably be assumed to represent the interests and activities of an individual. It is then possible for researchers to extrapolate and interpret these data. Although handheld devices are not often currently used for m-commerce, wireless Web activity will increase exponentially in the near future. In that event, phone companies will have access to a positively staggering amount of personal data:

Location

At the most basic level, the company will know where the consumer lives. It's on the phone statement. But that's nothing new. What *is* new is that the company will soon be able to find customers no matter where they are and pinpoint their *exact* location, within a few hundred feet. That opens up couple huge marketing angles. First, local businesses will be able to advertise only to people who live or work in the immediate area, so wireless could be a huge boon to small business. Second, many customers are given to impulse buys; people can be hit with an appropriate store ad or coupon when they are walking directly in front of the store. Such tactics could yield strong results.

Demographics

Along with location, cell phones and PDAs can also yield a detailed customer profile. Advertisers might be able to learn a subscriber's age, gender, ethnicity, and similar personal information. Such data would allow companies to send sharply targeted ads for a single product to the ideal demographic. Only young men would receive video game ads, for example.

Purchasing Profiles

In the near future, people who pay with cell phone accounts will be accumulating a stockpile of statistics for the phone company. Marketers might learn what they buy, how often, at what price, and in what combinations.

They could then use the information to even more selectively target the most receptive audience for a coupon or ad.

Constant Access

Not only might companies have a thorough familiarity with customers' lifestyles, but they will also have a near-constant access to their clients. Most handheld owners carry their PDAs and/or cell phones around on their person, in a pocket, purse, or briefcase; they also usually have them switched on most of the time. Therefore, if a marketer wants to send an ad that's applicable for only a short period of time, the marketer can do so in the knowledge that most of the recipients will notice the ad within minutes.

Dangers of Wireless Marketing

When many people first hear about the potential of wireless advertising, they become either uneasy or angry. They resent the noticeably increasing power of the corporation or business, and they fear that this power will be abused. And here's the bottom line: They're right to feel anxious. Wireless marketing can be highly dangerous. The very knowledge and access made possible through mobile computers can become a vehicle for privacy violations and harassment.

Privacy Violations

Most consumers do not like the idea of a Big Brother-type company that knows everything about them. Not only is it rather creepy to think that some faceless executive knows you like bananas, but it can also be frightening. Thieves or other unscrupulous individuals might use the demographic or lifestyle data to steal money or property or even to harm someone. Privacy rights, then, are a vital issue in the wireless arena. It is very important for all companies to take this issue seriously; mishandling sensitive information can have serious repercussions.

Harassment

On a slightly less serious note, mobile advertising can be used too often, to the point where it becomes harassment. Phones and PDAs are like e-mail boxes, in that they are a customer's personal link to the outside world. The appearance of a long series of advertisements popping up on the screen would be highly resented by most anyone, the same way consumers resent spam on the wired Internet. In fact, wireless spam is even worse, because it insinuates itself upon the recipient. Spam waits patiently for you to log on. Unwanted wireless ads beep at you, almost the second they reach the device. They seek you out and demand attention, and that's not necessarily a good thing.

So: How often is too often? Well, it depends upon

the individual. For some, even once would be more than enough. Other people are comfortable with a fairly high rate of wireless ads. We talk about this further in just a bit.

The Wireless Opportunity

Wireless advertising isn't all darkness and despair, however. In fact, if you know how to toe the line, you'll have the fabulous opportunity to both expand your customer base and help you provide better service. Mobile marketing done well has the potential to increase your profits and please your clients—which isn't half bad!

For Customers

Customers will be served better and more completely. They'll have the opportunity to receive an offer when they want it and where they need it—and without having to expend any effort whatsoever. Consider the following situations, in which timeliness and simplicity play important roles:

- A customer shopping in a grocery store receives an electronic coupon that grants him $1 off a favorite food item.

- An exhausted person driving late at night receives an ad for a nearby hotel, along with a discount and a link for directions. Anyone who's ever been lost and exhausted at midnight can appreciate the value of that particular offer!

Both of these situations show how mobile computers can actually improve the way the public perceives a business; clients might come to see the business as helpful, perhaps even thoughtful. Indeed, good wireless ads can make any consumer's life more convenient—and less expensive.

For Companies

Of course, the whole point of an advertising campaign is to benefit yourself as well. Happily, recent studies suggest that businesses stand to gain a great deal from wireless advertising. Listed here are only some of the most salient benefits:

- **Increased impulse buys.** Because you're able to reach customers on the spot or in transit, you're more likely to catch them at an opportune moment where an item they want is both in plain sight and easy reach. It's tough to window shop, but it's even tougher to deny the impulse when a coupon or a two-for-one offer is staring you right in the eye.

  This is especially helpful to smaller companies that focus on their brick-and-mortar presence. Perhaps you run Internet ads, but customers often won't bite unless they can buy it online. After all, they're too tired to run out to the store for whatever you're offering—and by the next day, they've squelched the desire. (Rats!) Wireless ads have the potential to turn a lot of "wants" into purchases.

- **Getting your name way, way out there.** Outreach isn't just about impulse shopping—it's about finding the customers that won't otherwise find you. With wireless technology, you're better able to reach customers when they're away from local areas. People can't always plan for what they're going to *need*—the situation occurs suddenly, and the customer needs immediate attention. A wireless Yellow Pages can list your restaurant for a customer looking for an authentic Italian place in an unfamiliar neighborhood—boom! A customer that you wouldn't have otherwise had. And if the customer lives close enough to the restaurant and you served a terrific meal, you might have made a repeat customer. The same goes for movies, or barber shops, or convenience stores.

....
With wireless technology, you're better able to reach customers when they're away from local areas.
....

- **High response rate.** Some of the earliest wireless ad studies have returned fantastic results. The percentage of people who respond to the ad frequently runs to about 4 percent or 5 percent. In one instance, the Ericsson telecommunications company received a 20 percent response rate to various ads they sent to Internet-enabled phones! (As a comparison, traditional Internet banner ads garner only about a 1 percent click-through rate.) Sure, some of the warmth is the result of the novelty of the service. But the numbers are still difficult to ignore, especially when standard Internet advertising has become so lackluster. Besides—they're cheap, which leads us to . . .

- **Low costs.** Wireless ads are dirt cheap, even cheaper than banner ads. They're so simple that it takes very little time to create them, and distributing them is as easy as selecting a list and pressing a button. If for no other reasons, wireless ads are worth a try simply because they're so very inexpensive. Why not?

In almost any situation, wireless advertisements are a dream come true for companies. They can dramatically increase revenues while barely putting a dent in your fiscal pocket. The only caution revolves around moderation and treading carefully, because an overly aggressive campaign will alienate customers—and that will only lose you money in the long run.

Wireless Marketing in the Real World

The most prevalent forms of future wireless marketing are still being discussed by experts around the world.

The Look

Even the most experienced pundits can't agree on whether wireless ads will eventually fall into the same patterns as traditional Internet ads. Some of them insist that cell banners will soon be as commonplace as those on the desktop at home, but that prediction has yet to be borne out. After all, the average screen size of a cell phone is always extremely pressed for space; trying to squeeze a pop-up ad in with the actual content would be like trying to stuff a bear into a phone booth when there's already one inside!

At its heart, the debate comes down to whether the public will pay for wireless Internet access. If customers continue to pay for wireless access, then they will resent having to wade through any advertising. If the wireless Web becomes free, then people will probably be more willing to tolerate the inconvenience of ads. Right now, most people are still willing to subscribe and pay extra, but others say that it won't be long until people begin to clamor for free access.

Japan seems a likely model, since by late 2001 it had gone farther with the wireless Internet than any other country in the world. In Japan, remember that phone users subscribe to imode for only a few dollars per month. After that, they pay for service according to the amount of material that they download. This seems a likely scenario even for other countries. Right now, wireless surfers in the United States pay for their time per minute, which discourages them even more from browsing or looking around. In Japan, users pay only for what they take; their access is constant, thanks to the packet-switched system. Nevertheless, they still pay. The wireless Internet is not likely to be a free commodity, at least in the foreseeable future. If the Japanese example spreads to the rest of the world, then those familiar, passive Internet ads, such as wireless banners and pop-ups, will never become as popular on handhelds as they are online. That means that companies need to be careful—and be creative.

> Given the "always on" nature of handhelds, a single marketer can find any number of people with the touch of a button.

"Push" Marketing

The wireless marketing world, then, will probably come to focus on "push" marketing. Push marketing is characterized by an active approach; rather than sitting and waiting for the customer to find it, it finds the customer. Mobile computers are uniquely suited to this technique. Given the "always on" nature of handhelds, a single marketer can find any number of people with the touch of a button.

There's also a slightly less aggressive approach; you could program your mobile site to issue an e-coupon or discount at the exact moment someone *accesses your own Web site*. This method combines the immediacy of a wireless ad with the assurance that—at that moment—the customer was interested in hearing more about the company or your products. In this situation, the surfer is not at all likely to be annoyed; in fact, you may very well convince the person to visit your store or to make a purchase on the spot.

Regardless of which type of ad you'd like to try, you

still need to make sure that you're not shooting yourself in the foot. Customers are sensitive, so the ads need to be created very, very carefully. Whenever you design a wireless ad, you should strictly adhere to what we call the "Three T's." Check that your ad is:

- **Targeted.** Be selective. This is, by far, the most important requirement. In the first place, your customers must have previously chosen to be on your mailing list; they *must* have opted in; otherwise, sending the ad is considered a serious breach of privacy.

  Second, you should send the ad only to the demographic group that's likely to be interested. You can include senior citizens in your video game discount mailer—maybe one of them will buy a unit for a grandkid—but then you risk sending too many ads to too many people. It's extremely easy to wear out your welcome on a tiny mobile device. Don't become a constant presence, or you risk alienating your audience. If you target only one segment at a time, you keep a lower profile and reap the maximum reward. You can always hit the senior population later, with a sale on golf clubs!

- **Trenchant.** Your ads must be both concise and compelling. Long-winded ads have no place on the wired Web, much less on a cell screen. Get right to the point. And what should your point be? You need to be offering customers something significant. If you're going to grab their attention for a moment, you need to make it worth their while. If customers receive irrelevant or misleading advertisements from your company, you'll be lucky if they merely ignore your ad; they might send an angry e-mail or even move to block any further messages. There is a very fine line between convenience and harassment. Be as sure as you can that your customers will want to click on your offer.

- **Timely.** Timeliness is a quality that we touched on previously. Wireless ads should ideally arrive at just the right moment—and they should never, ever arrive too frequently. So how can you work to avoid irritating people?

  The best way to ensure good timing is to try restricting most ads to specific situations. For instance, if a customer logs on to your mobile Web site, then you should feel comfortable sending that person a targeted offer. After all, by visiting your site, the customer has indicated a definite interest in thinking about your store at that very moment.

  Other nonaggressive forms of advertising can work as well. You can strongly market your company in the mobile Yellow Pages, or genre guides (such as a restaurant guide), so that people looking for your type of business in your area can find you easily. If they follow a link to your page, you can shoot them an ad. This is all advertising, but it's initiated by the customer as well.

In a nutshell, get your clients great offers—but do so on their terms and at their convenience. Be targeted, trenchant, and timely. Those are the keys to effective wireless advertising.

Customer Care

Wireless does far more than just put customers within constant reach; m-commerce also places your business on the hot seat. If you can always reach your clients, then they should also be able to reach you—24/7, if at all possible. You therefore need to ensure that you're taking full advantage of the mobile situation, working to constantly improve and upgrade your customer service. There are a few different practices you can try, the most innovative of which is click-to-voice.

> If you can always reach your clients, then they should also be able to reach you—24/7 if at all possible.

Click-to-Voice

Although PDAs are certainly widespread, no handheld has become as dominating a force as the cell phone. And, since cellular phones are voice-centric devices, you should consider adding voice functionality to your Web site. You can accomplish this by imbedding a click-to-voice option in your Web site—perhaps in more than one place.

> Since cellular phones are voice-centric devices,
> you should consider adding voice functionality
> to your Web site.

Click-to-voice is a painless way to notify a customer service department (or representative) that a customer needs help. When an individual is wirelessly surfing a Web site, he may have a question or concern that needs to be immediately addressed. Perhaps he wants to verify that a certain size is in stock or ask what specific seats are still available. In ordinary circumstances, he would have only two options: Either hang up and call the customer care hotline (which is included on every page of any good Web site) or e-mail the company.

Neither one of these choices is ideal. In order to call the hotline, the customer has to break the connection in order to use his phone, at which point all the information on the page he was looking at vanishes into the ether. He may then have to spend a number of minutes on hold waiting for a representative, and when one finally answers the call, it's possible that the caller will have forgotten some important fact. Of course, he could try writing it down in advance, but that's a hassle, especially if he's walking around the city or otherwise occupied with other tasks. Ugh. He has just spent several minutes trying to get an answer to one simple question, and when he finally has the opportunity, he has to explain everything to a representative who knows nothing of his situation—at which point he might be groping to remember the details himself.

Then there's the e-mail option. That's obviously not a great situation; no matter how fancy or cutting edge his cell phone happens to be, messaging and e-mailing are still a giant pain. Scrolling through numbers to enter letters also requires a great deal of concentration, and the customer may or may not be able to devote serious attention to the effort.

Click-to-voice solves these problems. In a click-to-voice option, the customer merely clicks on the appropriate button, then hangs up the phone. His phone number and customer profile are transferred wirelessly to the customer service department, along with a detailed description of the particular Web page he was looking at when he clicked. Instead of waiting on hold, the customer can get on with his life for the next few minutes; he is confident that the service rep will contact him as soon as possible. Sure enough, just a little while later, his phone rings. It's the representative, and she's ready for his question. She may know a bit of his customer history, she knows (at least in general) what he was looking at, and she's at his service. The customer can then have all of his doubts or questions resolved to his satisfaction, at which point he can either hang up or choose to have the service representative complete the sale. That's just about as easy and as painless as it gets. The customer gets excellent service on demand, and the company turns another profit.

Value Your Clients, One at a Time

It's not just about advertising. Mobile messages can be used to communicate with your customers on a more personal level, as well. If someone came to your auto shop for new brakes and a tune-up, for example, you might send the client a message in the next few days to make sure that everything went well:

```
Hey, Greg—
I just want to be sure that those new
brakes are working properly. If you're
experiencing problems, or if you have any
questions at all,
```

CLICK HERE

```
Don't forget that you're due for another
tune-up when you hit 31,540 miles.

Regards—
Mike
```

Or, if you run a flower shop:

```
Hi, Debbie!
I wanted to let you know that your
bouquet was delivered to Joe's door
```

```
at 10 A.M. this morning. If you have any
questions, or if you'd like to place
another order,
```

```
CLICK HERE
```

```
Talk to you soon!
Rebecca
Wildflowers, Inc.
```

Indeed, a proper follow-up message can work absolute wonders for your customer relations. In the first place, your customers will usually love the service. It makes them feel valued, and they appreciate the level of personalization and care. You can keep a solid hold on longtime clients and also increase the chances that a first-time customer will become a repeat customer.

It's also painless for you, the company. Wireless messaging is incredibly cheap; some companies send snail mail follow-up letters, but that can be expensive. Sure, e-mail is fine, but it also lacks the aura of attention that a wireless message can convey; it is also less immediate. With a wireless message, you can craft a great image while also saving on paper costs.

Finally, it's preventive. You can find out about and fix problems before they become messy. Customers are always more likely to forgive and forget a product or service problem if you contacted them first. People are reasonable, and they are usually mollified if you take their concerns seriously. Few customers become angry unless they feel that they are being ignored by a faceless company. When used carelessly, technology seems impersonal. It's your job to dispel that image. Remember, it's all perception.

Even if you decide to wait for the present and research the subject further, don't procrastinate forever. Mobile computers are the future, and it's in your best interest to seize the day while you can. Almost any company stands to benefit from the latest trends and should take serious advantage of wireless technology. It's your chance to both increase revenues and polish your company's image. Just remember to be moderate in your approach, and you're set for success!

Chapter 7

A Few Words on the Mobile Future

Okay, so we can't really predict the mobile future. Wireless technology is changing and advancing so quickly that it's difficult to foresee what our lives will be like in the years ahead. Sure, we could guess. After all, it seems that everybody else is giving fortune telling his best shot. Tech literature is chock-full of imaginary, futuristic days—most of which begin "Imagine a world . . ."—that then proceed to describe in detail how Bob can't seem to go sixty full seconds without using or consulting a wireless gadget, from dawn to midnight. But that would be no more or less valid than all the other conflicting expert opinions floating around. It's like trying to describe the weather seven days from today—nobody really knows for sure.

One thing of the few things that we *can* safely guarantee is that there will surely be surprises: gadgets we didn't predict, uses we never dreamed of, dazzling new technologies that burst suddenly into the public consciousness like fireworks. But the most important reality for the business world to face is far more mundane: Mobility, like wired access, is not going to go away. It will only become stronger in the years ahead, and the people who are comfortable with the technology will have a definite advantage over everyone else.

As mobile computers continue to penetrate the public consciousness, there are a few *general* trends that it's somewhat safe to expect.

Expect Momentum

The Internet didn't succeed in the mainstream until access reached an acceptable speed. What that teaches us is that no matter how engaging the technology, it won't attract large numbers of people until it becomes fast enough for efficient, everyday use. People like novelty, but it has to be practical. And mobile computing? It's getting very, very close to "fast enough." Wireless networking is spreading like wildfire, and the mobile Internet is finally finding its legs.

In the next few years, the wireless speeds we're currently getting are going to increase exponentially. As computers become faster, more people and businesses will find it useful to embrace mobility, which in turn will pressure others to do the same. Speed is directly linked to usage, and usage drives further development, which in turn encourages more speed.

Momentum.

Expect Convergence

Twenty years ago, calculators and telephones had very little in common. For the past several years, in contrast, cell phones and PDAs have been growing closer and closer together, assuming more of the same characteristics. Right now, the world is packed with an unbelievable variety of mobile gadgets. To be fully plugged in, a cutting edge businessperson needs a cell phone, two-way pager, PDA, laptop, MP3 player, and far more.

> In the next few years, the wireless speeds we're currently getting are going to increase exponentially.

As time passes, however, the need for half a dozen gadgets will disappear. A person will be able to accomplish the same tasks with only one or two mobile computers— perhaps just a handheld that combines cell phone/pager/ PDA/MP3 functionality and a laptop computer for networking and word processing. Five needs will shrink to two. Some clothing outfitters have been selling pants that have a million pockets to accommodate your pile of electronic handhelds. Don't expect that trend to last.

Convergence.

Expect Convenience

A lot of early mobile tech adopters are experimenting with the full range of wireless possibilities. As a result, for the next few years it's going to be difficult to decide what we *can* do with mobile versus what we *should* do. During the novelty stage, programmers and techies will doubtless engage in a lot of experimentation, which is perfectly natural. But, in order to be successful in the long-term, technology needs to make our lives easier.

> No mobile technique or device will survive for long unless it adds something valuable to our lives.

For example, it's going to be a long while before we find out what wireless advertising techniques will work the best. Until that time, marketers are sure to try all sorts of innovative and borderline-crazy schemes. Don't be surprised if you find ads popping up on your cell phone screen as you pass certain stores in the near future; also, you can expect that wireless spam will soon become a major concern. But these first, tentative efforts are just that—tentative. When the public either fails to respond or loudly protests, such campaigns will die a quick death. No mobile technique or device will survive for long unless it adds something valuable to our lives.

Convenience.

Expect Security

Mobile technology cannot prosper without the perception of security. If you think that it took a long time for people to feel comfortable with wired Internet security—or if you're *still* not comfortable—then you understand why this is a major issue. Wireless technology seems even less safe than desktop surfing. If cyberspace is scary enough, then the wireless Web is positively petrifying. Consumers won't risk their wallets or privacy online until software is sophisticated enough to protect them. Such programs are imminent, but the public must trust them before they can be truly effective, and that may take some time. The *image* of safety is equally as important as actual safety.

Security.

Expect Integration

Finally, the trademark of a mature technology is a feeling akin to boredom. In the early stages, when a gadget is still fresh, people can't stop talking about it, speculating, experimenting, writing articles, and trying to predict the future. New inventions always fully occupy the public consciousness—and that's where we are now with mobile computing.

Back at the beginning of the twentieth century, when automobiles were just starting to become popular, people were absolutely fascinated with them. Scientists wrote about the future of cars, owners took extraordinary pride in exhibiting their sleek status symbol—people even took them out for drives because, well, just because they *could*. And today? A car, for many people, is simply a form of transportation. The pure excitement of years past is largely vanished, now limited to a small segment of the population.

Eventually, wireless technology will reach the same point. Although it's creating a buzz—in which this book is fully participating—there will come a time when it's seen mainly as just another means to an end. The new tools will be important, true; and we will rely upon them for everyday business and communication. But a certain measure of the excitement will be gone. That's when mobile computers will have finally found a niche.

Integration.

A Comprehensive Mobile Glossary

Our promise to the reader: We don't believe in partial, incomplete glossaries. In a typical technical glossary, unexplained omissions or vague explanations leave novice readers with unanswered questions far too often. Not in this book. If it's a technical word, and if it was mentioned anywhere in this book, it's listed here.

Guaranteed.

10BaseT. A wired Ethernet standard that can process data at 10Kbps. 10BaseT is an older standard and thus has a lower data transfer rate. See also *100BaseT, Ethernet, LAN.*

100BaseT. A wired Ethernet standard that can process data at 100Kbps. 100BaseT is newer and faster than 10BaseT. See also *10BaseT, Ethernet, LAN.*

1G. Stands for first generation and refers to the earliest cellular phone technology. 1G phones are all analog devices and lack the ability to transmit data. See *analog.*

2G. Stands for second generation and refers to the advent of digital phone technology. 2G phones are capable of limited data transmission, usually at speeds of about 9 to 20Kbps. 2G phones are the current standard, although they are no longer cutting edge. See also *digital.*

2.5G. Stands for 2.5 generation and refers to the latest, most advanced digital phone technology. Such handsets are capable of transmitting data at speeds of more than 100Kbps and can also offer dedicated access. They represent the first truly convenient method of wireless Internet access. 2.5G phones are not common, but are being sold in increasing numbers. The 2.5G units represent a temporary bridge between older 2G and as-yet-unreleased 3G phones. See also *2G, 3G.*

3G. Stands for third generation and refers to the imminent wave of cutting-edge cellular technology. 3G phones will offer data transmission speeds of several hundred Kbps, perhaps up to 1Mbps in the next few years. They are still in the development stages and are not yet available in large numbers.

802.11. An early wireless local area network (WLAN) standard, developed in the 1990s by the Institute of Electrical and Electronics Engineers (IEEE). 802.11 is based on either FHSS or DSSS technology and permits a data rate of about 1 to 2Mbps. 802.11 can also designate a related family of 802.11 standards, such as 802.11b and 802.11a. See also *DSSS, FHSS, IEEE, WLAN.*

802.11a. The fastest 802.11 standard available, and also the most expensive. It can support a data rate of 54Mbps, which allows for a solidly functional business speed. WLANs still cannot match wired speeds, but 802.11a helps them get relatively close. See also *802.11, 802.11b, WLAN.*

802.11b. The most widely used 802.11 standard; despite its later position in the alphabet, 802.11b actually debuted a few years before 802.11a. 802.11b can support a data rate of 11Mbps. Although this is extremely slow compared to wired networks, 802.11b was the first wireless standard to make it practical for businesses to try going wireless. 802.11b has been adopted by the Wireless Ethernet Compatibility Alliance and is also referred to as Wi-Fi and High Rate. See also *802.11, 802.11a, WECA.*

Access point. See *wireless access point.*

Advanced Mobile Phone Service. See **AMPS**.

AMPS. Advanced Mobile Phone Service. AMPS is the analog cellular phone standard for North America. It was developed by Bell Laboratories in the 1970s, became widespread in the 1980s, and still controls about two-thirds of United States mobile telecommunications. It is now considered outdated in Europe but lingers in the United States for a variety of reasons. See also *TDMA.*

Analog. Analog is a method of wirelessly transmitting sound; it carries the signal as a voice wave. Analog was the simplest and earliest form of cellular communication; it was developed in the 1970s and first used commercially in Norway. Analog cannot be encoded and is thus highly vulnerable to both interference and eavesdropping. It is now considered outdated, having been supplanted by digital technology, but it is still widely used in the United States in the AMPS system. See also *AMPS, cellular, digital.*

API. Application Programming Interface. An API is a group of software interfaces that provide access to software functions. In other words, the API serves as the middleman between software (programs and applications) and hardware (e.g., computer or handheld).

Asymmetrical encryption. Asymmetrical encryption is the most effective and convenient method of encryption. In order to both keep the transmission secure and facilitate easy communication, asymmetrical encryption involves the use of two keys. The most popular system is Public Key Encryption, or PKE. See also *PKE.*

Bandwidth. The amount of data that can pass from sender to receiver in a given amount of time. Bandwidth is generally measured in thousands (K) or millions (M) of bits per second, or bps. As reference, standard home Internet access has bandwidth of about 56.6Kbps. The higher the bandwidth, the faster the flow of data, and thus the more speedy the transmission. See also **bit.**

Biometrics. Biometrics is the use of a unique human physical characteristic as a valid form of ID. Common biometric ID traits include fingerprints, retinal scans, and voice.

Bit. A binary digit, or one unit of binary data. Binary data, the most basic form of computer data, can be represented only by a 1 (meaning the electric current is on) or a 0 (meaning the current is off). At its roots, all computer processing is performed using only these two characters, which is why it's called binary. Bits are often used to calculate data processing speed; the more bits per second (bps) that a computer can handle, the faster the program. Bps is usually paired with different letters to represent varying speeds: Kbps represents thousands of bits per second; Mbps, millions; and Gbps, billions.

Bluetooth. A new and highly innovative type of Wireless Local Area Network (WLAN). Bluetooth was first developed by a far-reaching consortium of major tech companies that are interested in linking all kinds of computers and electronic devices, even appliances. Bluetooth was named for Harald Bluetooth, a Viking king who unified his kingdom, just as developers hope the technology will have a unifying effect on the electronics world. Bluetooth will enable computers to share information and commands with a wide variety of devices, from MP3 players to copiers to TVs. See also *WLAN.*

Bps. Bits per second. See **bit.**

Browser. A software program that is used to view documents on the Internet. It seeks, reads, then displays pages as they are requested from a server. Popular browsers include such giants as Microsoft's Internet Explorer. See also *server.*

Byte. One byte equals 8 bits of information. One byte can also represent a single character, such as a letter, typographical symbol, or number. A byte is not to be confused with a bit; they are distinct units. See also *bit.*

Carrier Sense Multiple Access/Collision Avoidance. Usually referred to as CSMA/CA. CSMA is the standard way networks, either wired or wireless, access communications channels; CSMA/CA makes a special allowance for wireless. In CSMA, the system first checks or "listens" to see whether the channel is clear, then sends a packet of data addressed to a particular recipient. In wired systems, the network can tell whether there was a collision between data and can resend the packet; in wireless systems, however, the network is deaf to collisions unless certain precautions are taken. That's where the Collision Avoidance comes in.

With Collision Avoidance, if the data are received, then the recipient node returns an acknowledgement, or ACK packet. If the CSMA/CA does not receive the ACK packet within a set period, it resends the packet. CSMA/CA thus ensures a high degree of transmission accuracy even in a WLAN. See also *packet-switching, WLAN.*

CDMA. Code Division Multiple Access. Developed by Qualcomm, CDMA is a spread spectrum cellular technology. It encrypts various data packets with a particular address and code, then sends them along various channels to the receiver. Once they reach their intended destination, the receiver reconstructs the message according to the directions encoded on each packet. CDMA is an efficient method of wireless communication, because it makes good use of scarce spectral resources. CDMA is widely used in the United States and is the launching pad for such 3G technologies as WCDMA and CDMA-2000. See also *CDMA-2000, channel, spread spectrum, WCDMA.*

CDMA2000. CDMA2000 is an upgraded, 3G version of CDMA. It offers a far faster processing speed—a maximum capacity of almost 4Mbps. It's directly competing with the imminent WCDMA standard. See also *3G, CDMA, WCDMA.*

CDPD. Cellular Digital Packet Data. CDPD is a way to send packet data over a single channel in an old AMPS network; essentially, it's an upgrade. With a CDPD overlay, even an analog network can become packet-switched. See also *AMPS, packet-switching.*

Cell. When it refers to telecommunications, a cell is a wireless coverage area. More specifically, it's the area that can be serviced by a single receiver and transmitter. Because cells are based on radio signals, their boundaries cannot be rigidly defined. Therefore, networks of cells are often represented as a pattern of overlapping circles. The word "cell" is the basis for the term cellular technology. See also *cellular.*

Cellular. Cellular refers to the wireless phone/data networks that are based on the cell layout. Although the term is technically generic, it is sometimes used to specifically describe older, analog wireless systems, in contrast to digital. See also *analog, digital.*

Cellular Digit Packet Data. See *CDPD.*

Certificate authority. Also known as CA. A certificate authority is a third-party company that is able to issue ID verification for Public Key exchanges. The CA guarantees that the private key holder, and thus the recipient, is who he says he is. The sender is thus protected from sending sensitive data to a fraudulent address. See also *asymmetrical encryption, PKI.*

Channel. A channel is simply any pathway through which a communications signal can pass. In wireless systems, however, this is usually a specific frequency or frequency range. See also *frequency.*

CHTML. Compact HyperText Markup Language. CHTML is the stripped-down version of HTML, designed for use in the more limited handheld environment. It has the advantage of still being accepted by the wired Internet, but it also lacks the flexibility of some competing options. Currently, Japan has been the most enthusiastic adopter of CHTML, using the language in its popular imode phones. See also *HTML, imode.*

Circuit-switching. Circuit-switching is the traditional use of a communications channel. In a circuit-switched system, the transmitter monopolizes the channel or circuit for the entire duration of the session. During this time, no other transmitter or sender can use that particular channel. Circuit-switching is simple, but it's also an inefficient use of resources. In wireless telecommunications, it is being rapidly replaced by packet-switching. See also *channel, packet-switching.*

Client. In an exchange between computers, a client is the device that requests information or functionality. A client itself has little information or power. See also *client-server, server.*

Client-server. Client-server is a computer structure in which exchanges are divided between clients, which request information, and powerful servers, which store and provide information. See also *client, server.*

Code Division Multiple Access. See *CDMA.*

Compression. A telecommunications technique that eliminates redundant data to increase the data transfer rate. Digital signals can be compressed; analog signals cannot. See also *analog, digital.*

CSMA/CA. See *Carrier Sense Multiple Access/Collision Avoidance.*

D-AMPS. Digital Advanced Mobile Phone System. See *AMPS, TDMA.*

Digital. Digital is a newer, more advanced method of wirelessly transmitting information. Whereas an analog signal can send only sound waves, a digital signal transmits coded numerical data, which allows for actual data transfer. The telecommunications industry is quickly shifting to all-digital networks. See also *analog.*

DoCoMo. Short for DO COmmunicate over the MObile network. Although it appears to be a strange acronym, *docomo* means "everywhere" in Japanese. NTT DoCoMo is the Japan's largest mobile service provider. It has constantly been in the vanguard of wireless technology and has developed such systems as the hugely popular local imode phone system. DoCoMo also embraced the 3G W-CDMA as soon as it became available. See also *imode, WCDMA.*

Dropped call. A dropped call is a cellular phone connection that is accidentally disconnected or lost. Naturally, this is an event that telecommunications companies are doing their best to minimize.

DSL. DSL is a newer form of Internet access. It provides the dedicated access of framework relay, but at lower prices.

DSSS. Direct Sequence Spread Spectrum. DSSS is a spread spectrum telecommunications method that transmits messages on many frequencies simultaneously. It uses multiple channels, but it also sends multiple copies of each data packet among the various chosen frequencies. DSSS is especially resistant to interference because there are several backups of each data packet. DSSS is thus used in the highly rated 802.11b WLAN. DSSS is not to be confused with FHSS. See also *802.11b, FHSS, spread spectrum, WLAN.*

E-commerce. Electronic commerce. The first wave of Internet-oriented market activity, which gained popularity in the mid 1990s. Not to be confused with m-commerce. See also *m-commerce.*

EDGE. Enhanced Data rates for GSM (or Global) Evolution. A 3G system upgrade that can boost 2G digital GSM and TDMA networks to much higher data rates—from the low 2G two-digit speeds up to about 384Kbps. Both TDMA and

GSM are pushing for the upgrade because it will allow them 3G processing power without having to completely change the existing telecommunications infrastructure. See also *2G, 3G, GSM, TDMA.*

Encryption. The coding or alteration of transmitted data, performed in order to maintain security. There are two main types of encryption: symmetrical and asymmetrical. See also *asymmetrical encryption.*

Ethernet. The near-universal wired LAN standard. The Ethernet was adopted by the IEEE and appeared in 1974 at a data speed of 10Mbps. Modern Ethernet networks can move at speeds of more than1Gbps. See also *IEEE, LAN.*

Extensible Markup Language. See *XML.*

FHSS. Frequency Hopping Spread Spectrum. A transmission standard in which the signal switches or "hops" frequencies in quick succession. The sender times the hops according to a preset pattern, and the receiver—given the pattern by the sender—synchronizes itself with the hops so that the transmission seems unbroken. Although FHSS was originally developed during World War II as a way to evade enemy eavesdropping, it is now used to prevent interference from other signals. See also *frequency, spread spectrum.*

Frequency. The number of wave cycles completed by a sound wave in one second. Different frequencies distinguish various signals; as a result, a single frequency can be thought of as a single wireless telecommunications channel. See also *channel.*

Frequency Hopping Spread Spectrum. See *FHSS.*

Gateway. A gateway is a special node that links two different networks. For example, a WAP gateway normally links the WAP network to the wired Internet network. Gateways translate and buffer varying methods of communication. See also *WAP.*

Gbps. Gigabits per second. One gigabit is one billion bits. Gigabits are currently the largest possible units used to describe data transfer speeds. See also *bit.*

General Packet Radio Services. See *GPRS.*

GIF. Graphics Interchange Format. The GIF format is used for simple computer graphics and images. Many wireless handhelds, such as imode phones, can support at least the most basic GIF images, although WML still does not support the format. See also *JPEG, WML.*

Global Positioning System. See *GPS.*

Global System for Mobile communications. See *GSM.*

GPRS. General Packet Radio Services. GPRS is a temporary telecommunications upgrade that raises a 2G network to 2.5G speeds. GSM is currently implementing this overlay in its networks. Many companies, however, have chosen to avoid the added expense, waiting instead for superior 3G technologies such as EDGE. See also *2G, 2.5G, EDGE, GSM.*

GPS. Global Positioning System. GPS is a satellite system that allows a designated receiver's geographic position to be pinpointed. GPS readouts generally include latitude, longitude, altitude, and time; because many people are unable to make much sense out of these readings, companies are currently developing more interpretation-friendly GPS receivers.

Graphical User Interface. See *GUI.*

Graphics Interchange Format. See *GIF.*

GSM. Global System for Mobile communications. GSM is the European telecommunications standard. At its most basic, it's a 2G digital circuit-switched system that can handle data rates of from about 9.6 to 14.4Kbps. Because GSM is nearly universal, Europeans are reluctant to surrender the system in the face of newer, faster standards. As a result, 2.5G or 3G upgrades are popular; these overlays do not interfere with the basic system—they simply enhance it. See also *2G, 2.5G, 3G, circuit-switching, EDGE, GPRS.*

GUI. Graphical User Interface. The physical environment in which an operating system is situated, and includes, for example, the graphics and icons a user sees after she boots up her computer. See also *OS*.

Handheld Device Markup Language. See *HDML*.

Handoff. The process in which a cellular tower "hands" a wireless phone call to a different cellular transmitter in an adjacent cell. Handoffs are performed when a caller is traveling; as she moves from one place to another, her signal becomes weaker to one tower and stronger to another. At a designated point, the tower in the original cell passes the signal to the new cell. Handoffs can be either soft or hard. See also *cell, cellular, hard handoff, soft handoff.*

Hard handoff. In a hard cell handoff, the cell towers try to time the handoff exactly, with the original tower cutting the signal just before the receiving tower picks it up. When it works, there's no noticeable break in conversation. When it is badly timed, there's either a gap in the signal or the call is lost entirely. Although hard handoffs are easiest, they're also more prone to such accidents. As a result, they are not ideal. See also *handoff, soft handoff.*

HDML. Handheld Device Markup Language. HDML was the first programming language developed specifically for the limited handheld environment. Instead of designing documents around "pages" of code, HDML created the concept of smaller "decks" and "cards." HDML, along with XML, was one of the two main influences in the creation of WML. See also *HTML, WML, XML.*

HiperLan. HiperLan is a series of European WLAN standards; they're competing with the IEEE 802.11 series of standards. Although it has been backed by powerful telecommunications companies, HiperLan is not likely to become particularly influential; it has split into too many competing subcategories that are incompatible with one another, which rather destroys the concept of "standard." See also **IEEE**.

HomeRF. Home Radio Frequency. HomeRF was an early WLAN standard. Although it gained some strong initial support,

802.11b debuted soon after and crushed it. HomeRF still exists in a few companies, but nobody doubts that it will eventually fade into tech oblivion. See also *802.11b, WLAN.*

HTML. HyperText Markup Language. HTML is the standard system of markup conventions used for Web documents. The code consists of a complex system of tags, which describe the appearance and format of the enclosed text or data. When browsers request a page from a server, they then interpret the code and display the properly formatted document. See also *browser, tag.*

Hz. Hertz. The most basic unit used to measure sound wave frequency. One Hz is equal to one cycle per second.

IEEE. Institute of Electrical and Electronics Engineers. (Pronounced I-triple-E.) The IEEE is an organization that encourages and systematizes developing standards for the computer and electronics industries. The IEEE is almost universally heeded and thus is very influential. See also *801.11, 802.11a, 802.11b, Ethernet.*

Imode. Imode is Japan's most popular wireless Internet service. It's also by far the world's most sophisticated wireless Web system. Developed and administered by NTT's DoCoMo, imode has captured a large portion of the Japanese Internet market. Imode phones have color displays and can download graphics, simple animations, and MIDI sounds. Users can shop, bank, navigate, and perform numerous other day-to-day tasks online from an imode phone. Imode phones work best with CHTML Web sites and are the language's most numerous supporters. See also *CHTML, DoCoMo.*

Infrared. See *IR.*

Interference. Interference is any force or obstacle that acts to degrade or destroy an electrical signal. Interference can range from mountains to thick walls to other electrical signals.

Institute of Electrical and Electronics Engineers. See *IEEE.*

IR. Infrared. Infrared light is measured at just below the frequency of visible light; it can be used to communicate wirelessly from one device to another, but it needs a direct line of sight. (That's why you can't use the remote to turn the TV off from upstairs.) IR is a popular method of synching two handhelds. See also *synchronization.*

J2ME. Java MicroEdition, or Java Lite. J2ME is the scaled-down, handheld version of Java. It still adds a great deal of power and functionality, but at a lesser level than standard Java. One way that J2ME has solved the pocket memory squeeze is by storing only the most essential programs on the handheld itself. The rest are requested from the server and used as needed.

Java. Java is a programming language developed by Sun Microsystems; it has far more muscle than does HTML; the language also includes a set of APIs that can perform all sorts of tasks. Java does require more power than normal programming languages, which is the main reason that Sun developed J2ME for wireless devices. Java programs can be run on any platform equipped with a Java Virtual Machine. See also *API, HTML, J2ME.*

Java Lite. See *J2ME.*

Joint Photographic Experts Group. See *JPEG.*

JPEG. Joint Photographic Experts Group. JPEG images are more complex than GIF images; they are not yet good images to download to a handheld. WML does not support JPEG files, and few other phones can handle it, as well. See also *GIF, WML.*

Key. A key is a code system used to encrypt and/or decrypt a message. See also *asymmetrical encryption, encryption, PKE, PKI.*

Kbps. Kilobits per second. One kilobit is 1000 bits. See also *bit.*

LAN. Local Area Network. LANs include computers that are networked on a smaller, or local, level. They are usually in proximity, within a building, office suite, or home. The network connects them to one another through a system of wires or wireless signals. In the latter case, they are referred to as WLANs. See also *WLAN.*

Latency. Latency is the amount of time it takes for a bit of data to pass through a network to its destination. The longer the time, the greater the latency, and thus the slower the network. Latency is extremely undesirable.

Local Area Network. See *LAN.*

MAC. Media Access Control. MAC is a security feature offered on some WLANs. With MAC, authorized computer addresses are entered into a wireless access point. Unless a user has his MAC address on the list, he won't be able to access the WLAN. See also *wireless access point, WLAN.*

Mbps. Megabits per second. One megabit is 1 million bits. See also *bit.*

M-commerce. Mobile commerce. The newest wave of Internet-oriented commerce. M-commerce is focused on transactions and the exchange of information between the Internet and wireless computers—hence, mobile commerce.

Media Access Control. See *MAC.*

Messaging. Also called texting. Sending wireless text messages from one wireless device to another. See also *SMS.*

MIDI. Musical Instrument Digital Interface. The most stripped-down sound file possible on the Internet. MIDI files play only simple, tinny-sounding electronic melodies. Still, MIDI files, no matter how basic, are supported by only a few Internet phones, such as the technologically superior imode phones. See also *MP3.*

Mobile commerce. See *m-commerce.*

MP3. Motion Pictures Expert Group-1 Audio Layer 3. MP3 files are complex musical files that can be stored on and downloaded from the Internet. The music is high quality, and so it can be downloaded by handheld devices only with great difficulty. Still, given the popularity of MP3 files in the wired world, MP3 downloads will become commonplace once the wireless data transfer rates increase sufficiently. Besides, many handhelds—PDAs, for example—can easily play MP3 files that have been previously downloaded and stored on a separate disk. See also *MIDI.*

Motion Pictures Expert Group–1 Audio Layer 3. What are you doing looking here? Run, do not walk, to the simple *MP3.*

Musical Instrument Digital Interface. See *MIDI.*

Network. A network is a system of at least three electronic devices that can communicate with one another.

Node. A node is anything connected to a network.

Noise. Noise is any undesirable electric signal. Often referred to as *static.*

OFDM. Orthogonal Frequency Division Multiplexing. OFDM is a transmission technique in which the sender broadcasts multiple parallel streams of data on separate frequencies. Because OFDM divides a high-speed stream into several lower-speed streams, the level of interference is far lower, thus paradoxically increasing the rate at which data can be transmitted intact. The OFDM data rate is higher than with wireless spread spectrum technology. OFDM is the flagship for the 802.11a WLAN standard. See also *802.11a, spread spectrum, WLAN.*

Orthogonal Frequency Division Multiplexing. See **OFDM.**

OS. Operating System. The software that provides a computer's environment: the GUI, the basic programs, and so on. The OS is a system's framework. See also *GUI.*

Operating System. See *OS.*

Packet. A small amount of data in a packet-switched network. All packets are encoded with their intended destinations so that the system routers can properly deliver them independently of one another. See also *packet-switching.*

Packet–switching. Packet-switching is a system created to more efficiently transmit data over scarce spectrum. Unlike circuit-switched networks, packet-switched versions do not monopolize a channel or frequency while transmitting a signal. Instead, the channel is occupied for only as long as it takes to deliver the packet. This systems allows many users to share the same frequency, with only a minimum of slowing. See also *channel, circuit-switching, frequency, packet.*

Paging. Paging is a wireless communications system used for transmitting brief text messages. Pagers can be either one-way or two-way; the RIM BlackBerry is the best example of the latter. See also *messaging.*

PAN. Personal Area Network. The term PAN was coined in reference to the terms WAN and LAN. The difference is that a PAN is on an even smaller scale than LANs; it refers to the network established for a single person. PANs will be made possible largely through Bluetooth technology, which will allow an individual to have multiple wireless devices linked into a small, truly Personal Area Network. See also *Bluetooth, LAN.*

PC card. A PC card is an add-on computer card that lends additional functionality or features to a desktop or laptop computer. The specific programs introduced depend on the contents of each individual PC card.

PCS. Personal Communications Service. PCS is a generic name for any digital telecommunications service, particularly one that uses the TDMA system. Contrary to popular belief, the acronym PCS is not owned by Sprint. See also *digital, TDMA.*

PDA. Personal Digital Assistant. The term PDA encompasses pretty much any handheld, multipurpose computer that serves mainly as an electronic organizer. The most recent PDAs include a large number of other functions, including faxing, e-mailing, scanning, downloading programs, and wirelessly surfing the Internet. The most common types of PDAs are the Palm series.

PDC. Personal Digital Cellular. PDC is the wireless telecommunications standard used in Japan. It employs TDMA digital technology and is based on the American D-AMPS. PDC is ubiquitous in Japan but isn't likely to find anything other than local success. European and American standards are too well entrenched. See also *D-AMPS, digital, TDMA.*

Personal Area Network. See *PAN.*

Personal Communications Service. See *PCS.*

Personal Digital Assistant. See *PDA.*

Personal Digital Cellular. See *PDC.*

Piconet. A piconet is a Bluetooth WLAN composed of no more than eight distinct devices. Each device in a piconet can communicate directly with all of the others, although they play different roles: master or slave. Master devices initiate and control exchanges, while slave devices are passive, receiving data and performing tasks as directed by the master. (Still, the slave has the power to refuse the pairing.) See also *Bluetooth, scatternet, WLAN.*

PKE. Public Key Encryption. Public Key Encryption is an asymmetrical encryption process that uses two keys: public and private. The public key is available to anyone and is used *only* to encode a message. Once the message is encoded, it can be decoded *only* by the owner of the private key—that is, the person to whom the message is sent. In this way, even a first-time asymmetrical exchange is completely secure. See also *asymmetrical encryption, certificate authority, PKI.*

PKI. Public Key Infrastructure. PKI is the structure on which the Public Key Encryption system is based. It involves the use of both PKE and the CA (Certification Authority); the former facilitates the coded communications, while the latter verifies the identity of the recipient. See also *asymmetrical encryption, certificate authority, PKE.*

Port. A port is any docking point at which a computer connection can be made.

Protocol. Protocol is a set of rules or standards that govern a network or communications between different devices.

Public key. An encryption key that is available to the general public. See also *PKE.*

Public Key Encryption. See *PKE.*

Public Key Infrastructure. See *PKI.*

Pull advertising. Pull advertising is a prompted ad in which the customer makes a request or expresses interest in the product. See also *push advertising.*

Push advertising. Push advertising is an active ad directed at the customer; it is not requested but offered. See also *pull advertising.*

Scatternet. A scatternet is a Bluetooth network that is composed of more than one distinct piconet. Usually this develops because there are more than eight devices in a given area. In a scatternet, individual devices may or may not be able to see one another directly. Nevertheless, they can still communicate. See also *Bluetooth, piconet, WLAN.*

Server. A server is a powerful computer that both stores information and provides data and programs to clients that request it. See also *client, client-server.*

Service Set ID. See *SSID.*

Short Message Service. See *SMS.*

Smart card. A small plastic card that is capable of storing and processing data. Smart cards can be used as a form of ID, as a wallet (they store electronic cash), or even movie tickets. All of these uses, of course, depend on a supportive environment. Currently, the United States does not offer many opportunities for people to use smart cards; they're more popular overseas.

Smartphone. Another term used to describe multifunction wireless phones; they must be digital, with at least minimal messaging and data processing capabilities. See also *digital.*

SMS. Short Message Service. SMS is a mobile phone service that allows users to send and receive short electronic messages on a wireless network. SMS is very popular in Europe. See also *messaging.*

Soft handoff. A soft handoff occurs when a cellular tower in one cell waits for the other tower to establish a firm hold on the transmission before it cuts its own connection. Soft handoffs are clearly superior to hard handoffs, but they're also more difficult to execute. See also *cell, handoff, hard handoff.*

Soft key. A soft key is an unlabeled key usually found on WAP-enabled cell phones, often located just below the display screen. The key assumes whatever function is assigned to it by the program or WML document in use, from BACK to ACCEPT. The assigned function is displayed at the bottom of the cell's screen, just above the appropriate soft key.

Spread spectrum. Spread spectrum is a relatively secure method of wirelessly transmitting a data stream. In a spread spectrum system, data packets are spread over a wide variety of frequencies or channels, which minimizes interference. It is also more difficult for outside parties to intercept and translate spread spectrum signals. The two most common methods of spread spectrum transmission are DSSS and FHSS. See also *DSSS, FHSS, frequency.*

SSID. Service Set ID. An SSID is a WLAN security feature that requires networked computers to ask for a wireless access point by name. In this way, casual passersby or workers in a neighboring office can't accidentally gain access to a WLAN. SSID comes on a special PC card and is thus easy to install. See also *PC card, WLAN.*

Symmetrical encryption. Symmetrical encryption is a fairly basic method of encrypting data. Information is coded using one key, then is decoded using the exact same key. Most encryption devices currently use asymmetrical encryption. See *asymmetrical encryption.*

Synchronization. When applied to mobile computing, synchronization refers to the sharing of information between either a handheld device and desktop or two handhelds. Synchronization, variously called syncing or synching, can be performed either with a line-of-sight connection between IR ports or with a WLAN technology such as Bluetooth. See also *Bluetooth, IR, WLAN.*

Tag. A tag is a label used in computer languages to describe data in some fashion. Tags are usually represented in pairs, one to "open" the tag, another to "close" it. They can be easily spotted in documents, since they are always enclosed by brackets: < >.

TCP/IP. Transmission Control Protocol/Internet Protocol. TCP/IP is the standard Internet communications protocol. The TCP manages the data, while the IP portion of the phrase moves it; the IP reads address and directs the previously formed data packets. Together, they provide the framework and rules of Internet communication.

TDMA. Time Division Multiple Access. Also known as D-AMPS. TDMA is a digital wireless access protocol in which packets of data are consigned to extremely specific time slots. The system was created to minimize interference while still allowing myriad signals to share the same band of frequencies. TDMA is extremely common in the United States. See also *AMPS, digital, frequency.*

Texting. See *messaging.*

Thin client structure. A thin client structure is one that is stripped down to accommodate a limited programming environment, such as that on a handheld computer. Instead of storing complex programs locally, it stores them on the server, and the client device accesses them from a distance. A thin client structure conserves precious space, since only vital programs are stored on the handheld device.

Throughput. Throughput is the amount of data that can be passed through a particular channel in a given amount of time. The higher the throughput, the faster the data stream. See also *channel.*

Time Division Multiple Access. See *TDMA.*

Transmission Control Protocol/Internet Protocol. See *TCP/IP.*

UMTS. Universal Mobile Telecommunications System. UMTS is the 3G European network that will rely upon WCDMA technology for speed and sophistication. People often use the terms WCDMA and UMTS interchangeably. See also *3G, WCDMA.*

Universal Mobile Telecommunications System. See *UMTS.*

Universal Serial Bus. See *USB.*

USB. Universal Serial Bus. A USB is standard port found on virtually all desktop and laptop computers. It allows a number of auxiliary devices—for example, a mouse and a joystick—to link serially, plugging one into the other, thus monopolizing only one port. It's universal because the devices do not need to be of a particular brand. A "bus" is merely a device that enables connections. See also *port.*

Virtual machine. A virtual machine is a software interpreter that translates programs from a language unfamiliar to the CPU to one that is familiar. The Java virtual machine is the best known example; it can translate Java into just about any local computer language, thus making Java itself practically a universal language, as long as the unit itself contains a Java virtual machine. See also *Java.*

Voice Extensible Markup Language. See *VoiceXML.*

Voice recognition. The automatic conversion of spoken language into computer code or text. Voice recognition is gaining rapidly in popularity because of the voice-centric handheld environment. Cell phones could especially benefit from voice recognition technology.

VoiceXML. VoiceXML is a computer language based on XML; it can tag and transport programs and applications that employ a voice interface. VoiceXML can be written just like any other standard Web document and downloaded the same way. VoiceXML is a big deal because it allows complicated voice programs to be imported and exported from nonnative devices. See also *XML.*

W3C. WorldWide Web Consortium. The W3C is an international consortium formed in 1994 by a number of large Internet corporations. It was created to foster and establish universal Internet communications standards and protocols, such as TCP/IP, IP, and HTML. The W3C seeks unity and harmony in cyberspace programming.

WAN. Wide Area Network. WANs are a collection of local networks that are linked, usually by a universal entity such as the phone company. WANs are irregular in which terminals they include; WAN neighbors may include people in the same room or even in different countries.

WAP. Wireless Application Protocol. WAP is a seven-layer wireless protocol developed by the WAP Forum in 1997. It was designed to both systematize wireless communication and minimize its limitations. WAP dictates and supports standards that include wireless security measures, special handheld languages such as WML, and transport protocol. WAP is most powerful in Europe, and its standards are backed by hundreds of influential telecommunications companies. See also *WML.*

Wavelength. The distance between one point on a wave (the crest perhaps) and the same point on the next wave. A wavelength is also equal to one cycle of the wave.

WCDMA. Wide-band Code Division Multiple Access; also known as IMT-2000 direct spread. WCDMA is the most prominent of the world's 3G telecommunications standards. It's an improvement on CDMA technology and offers high-speed data transfer rates. WCDMA is a direct rival of CDMA2000. See also *3G, CDMA, CDMA2000.*

WECA. Wireless Ethernet Compatibility Alliance. WECA is an organization that was founded by a group of telecommunications corporations to standardize and certify WLAN protocols and products around the globe. If an 802.11b product is approved as interoperable with other 802.11b products, then it is referred to as Wi-Fi. WECA is not currently backing 802.11a. See also *802.11a, 802.11b, WLAN.*

WEP. Wired Equivalent Privacy. WEP is a security feature used in WLANs. WEP, which is a necessary feature of all Wi-Fi hardware, encodes each data packet before it's sent. The level of encryption can vary, from a standard 40-bit encryption to an almost uncrackable 128-bit version. See also *encryption, WLAN.*

Wide Area Network. See *WAN.*

Wideband Code Division Multiple Access. See *WCDMA.*

Wired Equivalent Privacy. See *WEP.*

Wireless access point. A wireless access point is a node in a network that provides high-speed access to the Internet and/or the WLAN. See also *node, WLAN.*

Wireless Application Protocol. See *WAP.*

Wireless Ethernet Compatibility Alliance. See *WECA.*

Wireless Markup Language. See *WML.*

Wireless Web. The wireless Web simply refers to the use of radio frequencies to access the standard World Wide Web, although many Internet pages are specially designed for wireless access.

WLAN. Wireless Local Area Network. WLANs are the exact same thing as traditional Ethernert LANs, only without the wires. With the latest technology, WLANs can current transmit data at speeds up to 10Mbps, although much higher rates are expected in the near future. The current discussions revolving around WLANs concern which standard or standards will survive the cutthroat competition. Bluetooth is a special kind of WLAN. See also *802.11, 802.11a, 802.11b, Bluetooth, Ethernet, LAN.*

WML. Wireless Markup Language. WML is a blend of the XML and the HDML programming languages. First, it preserves a stripped-down, handheld version of XML tags; WML tags denote content, rather than format, as HTML does. But WML also adapted the HDML design structure, using cards and decks instead of pages. WML is endorsed by the WAP forum, and most new Internet phones in Europe and in the United States can be described as WAP-enabled. Therefore, WML has become a very important language in a very short time. See also *HDML, HTML, tag, WAP, XML.*

WorldWide Web Consortium. See *W3C.*

XML. Extensible Markup Language. XML is a special markup language in that it uses tags to describe data *content,* rather than format, as HTML does. This allows for a great deal of flexibility; when variously structured handheld devices download an XML page, the tags give them enough information to make localized decisions about how to best display the data. XML also allows programmers to define their own tags, so new tags can be easily created as the need arises. XML was one of the two languages that gave rise to WML. See *HTML, WML.*

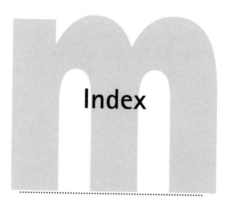

Index